Dedication

With tremendous gratitude I dedicate this book to Jesus for his great love, for Jesus is the Author and Finisher of our Faith! He is the fulfillment of all prophecy and when it is all over, we will be on our feet worshipping our Prince of Peace and King of Kings.

I also dedicate this book to my dear friend of 30 years, Patricia Ann (Patti) Wilde. I am sure the Lord Jesus when he walked on this earth was not as zany, swirky, flamboyant and sanguine as Patti "Poo"! I also know few people who loved Jesus with her same passion and exuberant style. She shared Jesus with everyone and never ended a visit or phone call without prayer.

One of the many things we shared was a love of music. Patti loved anything fast and loud. I can still see her hands flying over the keyboard, always ending her selection with a glissando. Since she refused to cut her beautiful nails, she often broke a nail on the finale and sent it flying through the air.

Precious Patti went to Heaven July 20, 2010 to be with her Lord and Savior—the Prince Charming of her faith. There she is healthy, happy, loved and adored.

Women who have lived wisely and well will shine brilliantly, like the cloudless, star strewn night skies and those who put others on the right path to life will glow like stars forever.
- Daniel 12:3 (The Message Bible)

I know my friend lived the dedicated life and influenced many for Christ. She is glowing like the stars forever in His presence. I am thrilled for my "forever friend" but I loved her and miss her greatly.

Until we meet again Patti, enjoy your new home.

Strategic Living In Strange Times

A STUDY OF THE BOOK OF DANIEL

PAULETTE BAKER PHILLIPS

Abba's House Publications
5208 Hixson Pike
Hixson, TN 37343

©2011 Ron Phillips Ministries

ISBN# - 978-0-9797268-4-2

PRINTED IN THE UNITED STATES OF AMERICA

Acknowledgments

If someone had told me ten years ago that I would write a book on Daniel and the prophecies contained in the scripture, I might have said, "That is not on the radar screen of my life–no way". Yet, as we are living in the strategic times of prophecy unfolding at break neck speed, I am compelled to put in print truths about the prophecies contained in the Book of Daniel and to communicate faith for the believers to live holy and wisely in these last days. When we see these strange things happening, we must look up to heaven for our redemption is very near.

I am thankful to the Holy Spirit for His prompting to teach this word. He ever draws me to Jesus and shows me that in that final day our Lord Jesus will come as King of Kings and Lord of Lords to reign supreme. So I have no fear of the future and neither should you.

For my dear Ron, I am thankful that you are my best friend and you have loved me for more than forty years of marriage and ministry. We have walked together in this fantastic journey: loving, learning and living a life of faith and worship. Without you I would have missed so much of the faith walk, for you have guided me, mentored me, and have even pushed me to be more. You have been my inspiration and my sounding board. Thank you for sharing your vast library with me and constantly encouraging me. I love you.

Thank you to my children Kelli and Kevin, Heather and Cain, and Ronnie and Kelly Nicole. You continue to bless my life. I love you all and I am so proud of each of you because of your faith and strong character. I am forever devoted to you all. You bring me so much joy because of my wonderful, perfect and amazing grandchildren you have given me. My seven grandsons and one granddaughter excite my life and give me joy and laughter every day. What delightful memories we are making. I love spending days spoiling and playing with Ethan, Owen, Collin, Max, Ava, Trey, Reid and Ryce. Your Gramee thinks you are all shining stars in her life and you can do no wrong.

I offer my love and appreciation to all those who are part of the Wednesday Haven Worship Service. We have studied together for twelve years and you have been faithful worshippers and prayer champions to me. You were the first to hear this teaching on Daniel and, as always, received the word with enthusiasm. After all this time, you probably know more than you want to know about me, but I pray you will always hunger to know more of God and his love letter to you–the Bible.

A tribute of honor is due to my friend, Angie McGregor, Executive Director of Communications at Abba's House, who went beyond the second mile to edit and help me in the final stages of the manuscript. Thank you for being devoted and tireless as you made this manuscript the best it could be. Thanks also to Sandy Watson and James Marler who provided extra eyes to make this manuscript readable. You provided literary abilities, insight and wisdom. To Doug Wright, thanks for your graphic design and formatting of the book. A big thank you to Julie Harding for her tireless efforts.

Thank you, Andrea Ridge, for typing the manuscript and giving it your full attention for many days. You were always gracious and encouraging along the way with your kind servant spirit. To my faithful friend and Administrative Assistant Denise Hamm, thank you for all you do for me each day. Your extra efforts with all the daily details freed me to work hours on end with this manuscript. I could not do what I do without you. Your godly example and your heart for ministry make us a great team. Andrea and Denise, you are both such valuable assets to Ron and me and the church family of Abba's House.

Contents

Forward

The people who know their God
shall be strong and carry out great exploits.
Daniel 11:32

Our God is full of all wisdom, honor, power and glory forever and ever.

He makes the nations rise and fall. He brings leaders to center stage and then removes and replaces them. The throne of our God shall be established forever in Zion and His righteousness throughout the earth. Our holy God is never defeated as we see in the prophetic book of Daniel, but He can be held at bay by human selfishness and willfulness. God's mercy and justice can be obstructed by human ignorance and lack of faith by believers.

Jesus himself said that He could do no mighty works among them because of their unbelief. This is still true today! Unbelief is rampant in many places across America and throughout the world. All is not lost because God can still accomplish great and mighty things through one yielded, believing individual. Don't forget David, a man after God's own heart who brought great victories for the armies of Israel. He brought down Goliath when the warrior army was paralyzed in fear.

In this book we will repeatedly see Daniel fiercely standing alone representing God to a heathen nation. His exploits and supernatural intervention from God shook more than one empire.

As you read this book, resolve within yourself to never consider retreat, but to forge ahead in love and passion for Christ.

Each of us has a unique and specific calling on our lives. No one else can be who God plans for you to be. Remember Daniel! Keep your eyes on Christ. He will send His heavenly forces to strengthen you and join you in every assignment. Do not constantly look for help from others, but look to God's presence alone. That is all Daniel had and that is all you need.

Do not be sidetracked by doubts or halted by fear. In the purpose of God you will find glorious victories and great exploits! Through your obedience you will bring joy to the Father's heart. Daniel was not influenced by the applause of Babylon, nor did he let the scorn of the jealous discourage him. Daniel walked with God and you can too. God will give you every support and encouragement you need as you seek Him and Him alone.

Historical Timeline

Biblical Events		World Events	
Creation	**Undated**		
Noah builds the ark	**Undated**		
Abram is born	**2000**	**2000**	**Native Americans come to North America**
Abram enters Canaan	1925		
Isaac is born	**1900**	**1900**	**Egyptians use spiked wheel**
Jacob and Esau born	1840		
Jacob flees to Haran	1764	1750	Square root understood
Joseph rules Egypt	1733	1700	Egyptians perform surgical procedures
Joseph dies	1640	1500	Sundial used
Moses born	1350	1358	King Tut buried
Exodus from Egypt	1280		
10 Commandments given	1279		
Israel enters Canaan	1240	1250	Silk made in China
Judges begin (Othniel, Ehud, Deborah, Gideon, Samuel, Samson)	1175	1183	Troy destroyed
Saul becomes king	1050		
David becomes king	1010		
		1000	Peking Built

Biblical Events | World Events

Biblical Events			World Events
Solomon becomes king, temple is built	970		
		950	Gold used as vessels and jewelry in Europe
Israel is divided into two kingdoms	930		
		900	Celts invade Britain
Elijah's ministry transferred to Elisha	848		
Elisha's ministry ends	797	800	Homer's Odyssey written
		776	First Olympic games
Amos's ministry begins	760		
Hosea's ministry begins	**753**	**753**	**Rome founded**
		750	Earliest written music
Micah's ministry begins	742		
Isaiah's ministry begins	740		
		700	False teeth invented in Italy
Northern Kingdom falls	722		
		660	Japan becomes a nation
		648	Horse racing at 33rd Olympics
Jeremiah's ministry begins	627		
First captives to Babylon, Daniel begins his ministry	605		
		600	Temple of Artemis built in Ephesus
Second captives to Babylon	597		
Ezekiel's ministry begins	593		
Judah falls, Jerusalem falls Solomon's temple destroyed. Jeremiah's ministry ends	586		
		563	Buddha is born in India
Daniel's first vision	553	560	Aesop writes his fables
		551	Confucius born
		550	Persian Empire started
Babylon overthrown by Cyrus, Daniel thrown to the lions	539	540	Horseback postal service in Persia

Biblical Events		World Events	
Cyrus' decree to allow exiled Jews to return. Second Temple construction starts	538		
		534	Tragedy a form of Greek drama
Temple work halted	530		
Temple work continues	**520**	**520**	**First public libraries in Greece**
Temple completed	516		
		509	Rome becomes a republic
		490	First short hair for men began in Greece
Ezra comes to Jerusalem	458	469	Socrates born
Nehemiah comes to Jerusalem	445		
Malachi last documented prophet of God until John the Baptist in AD 26	430	448	Parthenon built
		100	Julius Caesar born
		51	Cleopatra becomes Queen
BC / **AD**	0		
Jesus is crucified	30		
Stephen is martyred	35		
Paul's first ministry trip	48	43	London is formed
4 Gospels written	55–90		
Rest of NT written	50–95		
Second Temple destroyed	70	64	Rome burns
		75	Coliseum in Rome built
		570	Mohammed born

Clarence Larkin · Public Domain

Book of Daniel Timeline

The Exile & Babylonian Captivity

605 Babylonian King Nabopolassar (founder of the Chaldean Empire 605-562 B.C.) sends his eldest son Nebuchadnezzar II to defeat the Egyptians. On the way back from victory, they attack Judah, an ally of Egypt. The attack is cut short when Nabopolassar suddenly dies. His son rushes back home to ensure control of the throne. First deportation takes place (including Daniel, Dan 1:1).

597 Babylon attacks Judah; 2nd deportation (2 Kgs 24:8-16). King Jehoiakim dies. Jehoiachin reigns but is captive in Babylon for 37 years. Ezekiel is also brought to Babylon (Ezekiel 1:1-3).

587 Judah continues to be an annoyance, always ranting about Yahweh. Babylon loses patience and Jerusalem is destroyed; 3rd deportation takes place. The army occupies until 586 BC, destroying the temple, walls and gates. (2 Kgs 25:1-12; Psalm 137).

582 [estimated] Nebuchadnezzar II fails to acknowledge the one true God, suffers from insanity for seven years (Dan 4).

561 Nebuchadnezzar II dies, his son Amel-Marduk reigns (Evil-Merodach - 2 Kgs 25:27). King Jehoiachin is released from captivity.

555 Nabonidus reigns in Babylon. He is the last Chaldean ruler of Babylon. He spends the final ten years of his reign in Arabia (Teima) and leaves his son Belshazzar in charge of Babylon.

550 Cyrus II defeats Astyages, king of the Medes. The Medes accept Cyrus readily.

547 Cyrus II conquers Croesus, king of the Lydians.

539 Cyrus II takes control of Babylonia absorbing it into the massive Persian Empire. He decrees that the Jews may return to their homeland!

The Return from Exile & Reconstruction of Jerusalem

A small but loyal group returns. It **538** doesn't take long for their initial enthusiasm to run into tough circumstances. Everything had been destroyed: The Temple, the city walls, their homes. Foreigners had moved in. There is little commerce or infrastructure. Feeding their own families becomes a full-time, difficult task. Zerubbabel is political leader from the line of David, Joshua is high priest from the line of Aaron.

522 Darius I becomes King of Persia.

520 Temple founded. Work stops once obstacles arise. The Jews divert their attention to themselves. Two prophets, Haggai and Zechariah, motivate them to continue construction.

Temple completed! (70 years **516** after its destruction).

Second Temple Era

A small republic is established **510** in Rome.

485-465 Xerxes I King of Persia. His reign ends abruptly by his assassination in August. He was murdered by his own political aids.

Artaxerxes I Longimanus **465-424** rules Persia.

457 Ezra leads a second group of exiles to Jerusalem. He is known as a powerful scholar of God's law. He leads reforms dealing with foreign wives (& their false gods). While Ezra has grasped God's vision personally, he seems to lack the social and political savvy to inspire those around him.

Nehemiah, assigned as governor **445** of Judea, travels to Jerusalem (from Susa) with a personal mission to rebuild the walls of Jerusalem, which would serve to restore dignity and honor to the sacred land. Nehemiah has political clout and a strong vision of God's mission. He leads and inspires others. The walls of Jerusalem are re-built in 52 days, much to the surprise of surrounding hostile peoples.

END

Family Tree

Josiah, King of Judah

Middle Son
Ruled First

Jehoahaz
23 when he began rule.
Ruled 3 months.
Taken to Egypt & died.

Oldest Son
Ruled Second

Eliakim
**(Renamed by Pharaoh Neco
to Jehoiakim)**
25 when he began rule.
Ruled 11 years.
Killed back in Judah.
Body thrown over city wall.

Son of Jehoiakim
Ruled Third

Jehoiachin
18 when he began rule.
Ruled 3 months.
Taken captive to Babylon.

Youngest Son
Ruled Fourth

Mattaniah
**(Renamed by
Nebuchadnezzar to
Zedekiah)**
21 when he began rule.
Ruled 11 years.
Rebelled against Babylon.
Sons were executed
in front of him.
He was blinded and taken
back to Babylon.

Chapter One
A Life Interrupted

Then it shall be, if you by any means

forget the Lord your God, and follow other gods,

and serve them and worship them,

I testify against you this day

that you shall surely perish.

Deuteronomy 8:19

Imagine waking up to a disaster of epic proportions. Major cities full of business and commerce have been destroyed. The national government has been overtaken: no flag, no churches, no fair and unbiased courts, no currency, no schools, no national leader. You would never again visit a bank, sing "The Star Spangled Banner" in your homeland or sit in your worship service. Imagine the terror of children, now orphaned by violent terrorists, being carried off in chains. Could you survive? Would your faith in God be enough to sustain you for the rest of your life in a now foreign and oppressive land? Daniel faced a very similar situation and found that his faith in God was enough.

For the first fifteen years of his life, Daniel lived in the city of Jerusalem where he spent many hours in the synagogue, studying his heritage and immersing himself in the culture of Jerusalem under the guidance of his parents. He was highly intelligent and as a member of the aristocracy (with possible blood ties to the king), enjoyed a very privileged lifestyle. Clearly, he had many leadership attributes and an abiding faith in his God, qualities that would surely indicate a future filled with promise and blessings. But this was not to be, as one day suddenly the armies of Nebuchadnezzar stormed the city in the first of three sieges that would not only subjugate a nation, but radically change Daniel's life. During these attacks, all promising young teens, including Daniel, were captured and taken to Babylon.

While being held captive in Babylon, Daniel relied on his strong Jewish identity to provide the strength and perseverance necessary to survive. Not only did young Daniel survive his captivity, he thrived in the Babylonian culture.

Swiss-American Psychiatrist and Author, Elizabeth Kubler-Ross said, "People are like stained glass windows. They sparkle and shine when the sun is out, but when the darkness sets in, their true beauty is revealed only if there is a light from within." (1) The true beauty in Daniel's life was the inner faith and strong sense of heritage that sustained him nearly 90 years in a strange land. He survived because his faith in God was solid, unwavering and powerful.

In Daniel 9:23 the angel Gabriel came to answer Daniel's urgent prayer, exclaiming. "You are greatly beloved." Let us explore who Daniel was, why he received such high praise, and why the Holy Spirit inspired him to write this book.

At face value, Daniel did not appear to be a young man who was walking in the favor or grace of God. If he was truly "greatly beloved" by God, then why did he lose his parents, country, wealth, royalty and his homeland? Why was he held captive in another country, never to see his homeland again? Why was he tried in court many times and even cast into a den of lions? God's ways are not always our ways. Daniel was very special to God and was trusted with many difficult and enormous assignments. He was loved greatly and received abundant covenant grace.

Setting the Stage: Historical Background

The book of Daniel is not fiction. Events in the book of Daniel have been validated by historians and recorded as such.

The first six chapters of this book are God's plan for the Gentiles. And it is important to note that the first six chapters Daniel wrote were also a prophecy, as none of the events he wrote about had happened yet. Today we look back and call this history. The sign of a true prophet is that his or her words eventually become truth and events really occur just as he or she foretold. The last six chapters of the book of Daniel contain God's future plan for Israel. They deal with eschatology, the study of the end times.

All of Israel had followed other gods. Deuteronomy 31:17-20 and Deuteronomy 32:44 warned that God would forsake his people and allow their destruction if they served false gods. Punishment and chastisement did indeed come upon the nation during Daniel's tenure there.

King Josiah was a great king and reformer. He turned the people of Israel back to God and revival came to the nation, but not to the King's own sons. After the death of Josiah the younger son, Jehoahaz, ruled for only 3 months before being deposed by the Pharaoh of Egypt. The older son, Jehoiakim, ruled for 11 years. According to Jeremiah 36, 2 Kings 24:1 and Jeremiah 46:1, Jehoiakim was extremely wicked and under the thumb of Nebuchadnezzar. (Spelled Nebuchadrezzar by Jeremiah and Ezekiel). Jehoiakim rebelled against Nebuchadnezzar as did his son, Jehoiachin, after him.

2 Chronicles 36:4-8 states that Jehoiakim was taken in chains to Babylon by Nebuchadnezzar where he also carried the vessels from Solomon's temple to the treasure house in Babylon. Jehoiakim paid tribute to Nebuchadnezzar for the entire 11 years. He was murdered by Babylonian soldiers and his body was thrown beside the city wall without burial. Many Jews were taken captive and carried away from Jerusalem. The first siege was in

the 3rd year of Jehoiakim during which Daniel and other nobility were taken. In the third siege, all of Jerusalem was destroyed as was Solomon's Temple.

Isaiah 38:4-7 reveals:
• 605 B.C. Nebuchadnezzar carried off Daniel and his 3 companions with other youths and leaders
• 598 B.C. Nebuchadnezzar carried off Ezekiel
• 587 B.C. The Babylonians performed a complete holocaust and burned the city of Jerusalem and Solomon's Temple.

Babylon is the same place as Shinar mentioned in Genesis 10:10, where the Tower of Babel was constructed. In Genesis 11:1-4, 8-9, the Bible explains that it was in Shinar that the Tower of Babel was built from bricks by a united humanity of the generations following the Great Flood. God had instructed them to populate and subdue the entire earth. Instead they rebelled against God, desiring to be more powerful than He. So God confused the languages, dividing the nation into different people groups speaking different languages. In Genesis 12:1, the LORD said to Abram, "Leave your country, your people and your father's household and go to the land I will show you." Abram's country was the land of Ur. This entire area later became the Babylonian Empire. God had promised that He would defeat all the enemies of Israel as long as they worshipped Jehovah and had no other gods before Him. God had dealt very patiently with the Jews before He allowed their captivity by this massive world power. The Jews refused to repent and over time they assimilated into the culture of Babylon.

Because the city walls were 300 feet high and 80 feet wide, people could drive chariots on the top of the walls as if it were a freeway. The Euphrates River beside Babylon probably looked like the waters surrounding the city of Venice. The city itself was 60 miles square with each side of the square being 15 miles. Nebuchadnezzar had Hanging Gardens built for his wife, Amytis of Media, to remind her of her homeland. They were filled with lush fragrant plants that were native to Persia. Today, Nebuchadnezzar's Hanging Gardens are widely considered to be one of the original Seven Wonders of the Ancient World.

The temple of Bel, the pagan god, was 600 feet above the city. Comfort, pleasures, delicacies, wines, entertainment and sensual gratification were everywhere. This entire region was the breath taking and impressive Babylonian Empire.

About the Author

Daniel is the author of this book. He wrote it in Hebrew and Aramaic. Daniel 1:1-2, 4, 8:1-12:13 were written in Hebrew because these sections relate directly to the Hebrew people. Chapters 2:4b-7:28 were written in Aramaic for the world's informational purposes and future history. Daniel was of royal lineage and noble birth. He was born during Josiah's reign and lived at the end of a nation's life. He saw his beloved Judah destroyed. At the age of 15 he was taken into captivity, having been deported around 605 B.C. His captivity stretched for nearly 70 years. Daniel saw the fulfillment of God's prophecy on his nation. He heard the preaching of Jeremiah and Ezekiel and knew this was the judgment to come. Israel reaped a bitter harvest for her rebellion against God. Daniel saw his homeland fall to ruins and suffer the consequences of sin. He lived in a hopeless and dangerous time.

Daniel's Gifts

Daniel was carried to Babylon not to be a slave but to be reprogrammed and educated to become a statesman. He was born into royalty and an intellectual. Skilled in the social graces, he was very comfortable in the King's presence. But God gave him so much more. He was given supernatural abilities which allowed him to understand mysteries, dreams and visions. Ultimately at age 84, Daniel served under King Darius as one of the three presidents of all the satraps. Today, we might equate his role as one similar to that of the Prime Minister.

Daniel continued his leadership until the first year of Cyrus, which marked the return of Jews to Palestine. He lived his life with strong character, priceless religious convictions, accurate interpretations and appealing words of faith. His life span covered the entire epoch of the Jewish captivity. He witnessed it all and remained true to Jehovah. He was a true hero of the faith.

During his first three years of training, his integrity and overall performance were so far superior to those who were not worshipping Jehovah that he was heard and respected by a monarch who did not believe in the true God. Daniel understood that the kingdoms of this world were temporary, but the Kingdom of God would endure forever.

Daniel had the gift of prophecy but not the office of a prophet. What is the difference? Deuteronomy 18:18 explains that one had to be an Israelite to be a prophet. A priest represented the people to God and a prophet represented God to the people of Israel. Daniel's gift of prophecy was delivered to a pagan court and to the Gentile world. Daniel knew what would happen to the children of Israel. He knew God would fulfill his promises and keep his covenant of grace to his people (Numbers 12:1-8).

The Lord gave Daniel the ability to interpret the dreams of others and later gave him dreams and visions of his own, as well as their interpretations.

Daniel's Name

Daniel's name means "God is my judge."

Hananiah, a young Hebrew held captive with Daniel, means Yahweh is gracious –beloved of God. Mishael, another Hebrew captive, means "Who is like God is", in other words, there is no God like our God! Azariah, the fourth Hebrew mentioned in this text, means "Yahweh has helped or will help". Help is near when God is near.

These holy Hebrew names were changed to give credit to Babylonian deities. The idea was if you change a name, you control a person. The plan was to begin assimilating these captives from the first day of their captivity.

• Daniel's name was changed to Belteshazzar - prince of Bel
• Hananiah's name was changed to Shadrach - the sun god
• Mishael's name was changed to Meshach - like Shack or Ishtar
• Azariah changed to Abednego which means servant of Nego.
• Nebuchadnezzar means "Nebo protect or the protection of
  Nebo or Prince of Nebo. Nebo, the god of fire, was the chief god
  of heathen worship. Bel and Nebo were both pagan gods.

An attempt was made to blot out the memory of Jehovah of hosts, the God of the Hebrews. This was a subtle attempt by Satan to get rid of God. However, these new names were never used by God, the angels, Holy Spirit or the Hebrew youths themselves.

Daniel's Conviction

Daniel was a young man who did not forget his creator in the days of his youth. He was of great spiritual confidence. From the beginning of captivity to the end of his life, he never wavered or compromised his faith in God. What a testimony!

In our day, we should all be more like Daniel; however, young and old alike compromise and are rendered unfaithful and unholy. Godly convictions are cheaply sold to the low bidder where drugs, sex, and every imaginable kind of sin result in disgrace. Mature adults are just as compromised as the young and are setting very low standards for our next generation.

Daniel was a young man of dedication. Commitment meant something to him. Whatever God said do, he did without reservation or question in an age when his own people were disenfranchised in a foreign land, stripped of rights, privileges and freedoms. His life was marked by fasting and prayer. Daniel was in touch with God. Though not specifically stated in scripture, I believe his parents taught him how to pray and gave him a priceless spiritual heritage. How we have failed to prepare the coming generation to be godly and holy like Daniel.

The burdens of his new propaganda-filled studies and the demands of his position in court often sent him to his knees in prayer. The burdens of his devastated homeland and the poverty of his people grieved him to the point of intercession daily. Prayer was the key to Daniel's faithful life and it is also how we keep the faith- falling on our knees before our holy God. Neither Daniel's position at court, his prestige nor his outward purpose in Babylon ever kept him from God. I believe his life excited God. His faith was tested everyday. One such test was the food allowance for each day.

Daniel's Food

Babylon was the greatest city in the world at that time and could be compared to New York City today. While in Babylon, young Daniel was not tempted to do what the Babylonians did. Daniel's character and integrity were unchanged by his surroundings. They could change his name but not his nature.

When Daniel learned that he was expected to eat and drink everything from the King's table, he knew that he could not compromise his integrity. He sought a different way. Rather than cause a commotion through outright rebellion, Daniel's approach to the stewards was both humble and appealing. He had a gentleman's spirit and respectfully offered an opportunity to test his healthy diet against food from the King's table. He asked that he and his friends might be excused from the King's rich foods, delicacies and abundant wine. In addition to eating vegetables and water they also ate "pulse", which is similar to today's cereals or granola. The steward agreed to a 10 day test to see if Daniel and his friends might look as healthy as the other young men in the King's court. The feasts of the king at night were most often meat that had been sacrificed to their false gods. Their wine was a constant toast to the false gods of Babylon. In Eastern culture then and even now, to share a meal with someone is to make a commitment of friendship and family. Daniel was unwilling to partake of the covenant that the food from the king's table represented. Read Daniel 1:14-21.

God said, "Those who honor me, I will honor." (I Samuel 2:30) God honored Daniel. After 10 days of vegetables and water, he and his companions were healthier, brighter in complexion, stronger and blessed with great intellectual insight. The result was tremendous favor with the king. At the end of chapter one in verse 20, the King said that they were "ten times better than all the magicians and astrologers that were in all his realm." Because of this recognition, the young Hebrews were unchallenged for the duration of their three years of training.

Integrity is being the same person at all times and in all places, regardless of circumstances. Integrity is not swayed by who is around or what someone says. Integrity is being the same on the inside as you are on the outside. This character demands a consistency of behavior with no double standard or double minded thoughts or emotions. It is complete and undivided. It has been said that life is simpler when there are no costume changes. Daniel lived a life without costume changes. Babylon tried to steal his soul, but instead God protected him and poured out wisdom, grace, favor, knowledge and supernatural power upon him. Daniel had a God-centered world view. As a result, the world around him viewed his God, Jehovah. God is more concerned about character than popularity.

Daniel's Resolve

Without resolve it is easy for a person to lose integrity. Daniel resolved in his heart not to sin against his God. He purposed in his heart to live holy to the Lord. You can lose your integrity and purpose if you allow popular culture to rename you and indoctrinate you. The enemy tried to put a pagan exterior on Daniel and will try to do the same thing to us. But inside we can be full of God and His Word.

The entire 47th chapter of Isaiah deals with the humiliation of Babylon.

(8) Therefore hear this now, you who are given to pleasures, who dwell securely, who say in your heart, 'I am, and there is no one else besides me; I shall not sit as a widow, nor shall I know the loss of children';
(9) But these two things shall come to you
In a moment, in one day: the loss of children, and widow-hood. They shall come upon you in their fullness
Because of the multitude of your sorceries, for the great abundance of your enchantments.
(10) For you have trusted in your wickedness;
You have said, 'No one sees me';
Your wisdom and your knowledge have warped you;
And you have said in your heart,
'I am, and there is no one else besides me.'
- Isaiah 47:8-10 (NKJV)

The Babylonian culture was all about personal pleasures and security. They said in their hearts, "I am, and there is no one else who matters but me. I am the center of my world. I am the most important. I am entitled. I am perfect. It is all about me. I need extravagant, excessive and self-absorbed wealth and recognition." This was a culture, a philosophy and a lifestyle.

Life is not all about me, my, or mine. The cultural "I am" is not that important. Life is about the only real "I AM" and that is the Great I AM, Jehovah God. Daniel understood that truth and refused to be defiled by the culture's concepts.

We are confronted on every side by the corruptions of the world. I can only imagine my own children being taken away in captivity to Babylon like Daniel–oh, the grief. But our children and all generations ARE being taken away by a corrupt culture. The tactics we face today resemble closely what we see in Daniel, only without a physical war. It is perpetuated by greed, indoctrination and false gods. Where were the rest of Daniel's peers? There were many more young men and women in Babylon than Daniel and his friends Hananiah, Mishael, and Azariah. God forgive the unnamed majority, for they became anonymous and irrelevant and assimilated into the new "me centered" culture in Babylon.

I pray that we will repent as we see ourselves yielding to the tangled web of greed, material accumulation and entitlement. We must get Babylon out of the church and the hearts of believers.

Chaldeans & Shushan
Chapter 1 Appendix

The Chaldeans

Our first understanding of the word Chaldean comes from "Ur of the Chaldees". In Daniel's time, the word referred to an influential class, the top level of the five classes in Babylon.

The Chaldeans were always enemies with the Assryians. Nabopolassar, father of Nebuchadnezzar, was a Chaldean and Nebuchadnezzar's army was known as "the army of the Chaldeans." This group was not specifically Babylonian, although they often ruled Babylon.

Belshazzar is called "king of the Chaldeans." Herodotus tells that the Chaldeans were the priests of the great temple of Bel-Merodach-Esagila, or "the house of the towering summit." This was the place where Nebuchadnezzar housed the gold and silver vessels which were taken from the house of God at Jerusalem. This privileged and prominent upper class Babylonian life came to the forefront during the book of Daniel. It was those individuals who were jealous of Daniel's position and power over them. It must have been the Chaldeans who sneered and ridiculed Daniel, a foreigner, who was raised up to have power over them.

Shushan

Tradition tells us that the bones of Daniel are buried in this place. The southern portion of this mountain range is called Elam. These Elamites were enemies of Assyria. Sennacherib fought against them and nearly defeated them. But Elam recovered and in the end outlasted the Assyrian Empire. The Elamite forces joined with Naboplassar the father of Nebuchadnezzar to fight on the southern borders of Assyria. As Jeremiah foretold, Elam was attacked on all sides by the Babylonians and the Medes.

Shushan had been the royal capital of Elam and it became a strategic military outpost. In Persian times Shushan or Susa became one of the empire's capitals. In this beautiful city Daniel may have lived when he disobeyed the law and opened his windows to pray. This is the place where the prophet Daniel is believed to be buried.

Study  Guide

CHAPTER ONE • LIFE INTERRUPTED

Introduction

Even though we begin our study of this prophetic book with the captivity of a nation and a young teen, we also see the mighty hand of God on one individual who is totally committed to God throughout the captivity. In this awesome study of Daniel we will learn why the angel addressed Daniel with, "You are greatly loved." We'll explore who Daniel was, and why the Son of God inspired him to write this book.

1. In Daniel 1:1-2 write the names of the two kings and identify each:

1. _Jehoiakim King of Judah_
2. _Nebuchadnezzar King of Babylon_

2. Read Deuteronomy 31:17-21 and Deuteronomy 32:44 and tell why God allowed the destruction of Jerusalem and all Israel. _due to all their wickness in turning to other God_

3. The destruction of Jerusalem took place in three stages. What happened at each stage?

605 B.C. _Four hebrew children taken from Judah Daniel, Hananiah, Mishael & Azariah_

598 B.C. _Jehoiakim dead Ezekiel carried to Babylon_

587 B.C. _Zedekiah taken to Babylon, temple burned destroyed_

4. Find Jerusalem and Babylon on your map. Read Genesis 10:10 to find another name for Babylon. List them:

Babel , Ur

5. What do you know of Daniel's young life and background? _____

_____

_____

_____

6. Why do you think he wrote the book of Daniel in both Aramaic and Hebrew? _____

_____

_____

7. Explain his gift of prophecy and why it is different from the office of a prophet? _____

_____

_____

8.

Hebrew Name	Meaning	Babylonian Name	Meaning
Daniel			
Hananiah			
Mishael			
Azariah			

9. Have you ever been labeled with a "hurtful" or "bad" name? Remember the occasion and also how God gives us a new name in Revelation 4. List many names God speaks over us as His children.

_____

_____

_____

10. Compare the Babylonian culture to the Western culture of the USA. In what ways do both cultures try to enslave and cause Christians to compromise? _____

_____

_____

_____

11. What are some of society's pressures on Christians? _____

_____

_____

_____

12. Jeremiah, Ezekiel and Habakkuk were contemporaries of Daniel. What were the themes of their preaching? _____

_____

_____

13. How easily were you influenced at age 15? What about your son at that age? What makes Daniel so different from most teenage boys of this decade? _____

_____

_____

Can we live in an extravagant, excessive culture without being poisoned by it? Daniel and his friends proved by their integrity that this is possible.

14. What were the Babylonians instructed to teach Daniel and his companions? _____

_____

_____

15. What does the word "resolve" mean? What were some of Daniel's resolutions? How did God honor Daniel in Chapter One? _____

_____

_____

_____

16. Why did Daniel "resolve" not to eat from the King's table? _____

_____

_____

Daniel's resolve could have:
• Been an insult to the King
• Produced pressure from his friends
• Set them apart from everyone else and make them seem strange
• Jeopardize their chances of advancement
• Tempted them with gourmet delicacies which were the best in the world

17. What was the result of their committed resolve NOT to eat the food from the King's table? _____

_____

18. Write a definition of integrity. _____

_____

19. Consistent living protects our integrity. Read the following and tell how Daniel was victorious before God with his integrity preserved.

Daniel 2:22 _____

Daniel 2:47 _____

Daniel 3 _____

Daniel 4 _____

Daniel 4:35-37 _____

Daniel 5:23 _____

Daniel 6 _____

20. Daniel had unswerving loyalty to God and an uncompromised life. Is it possible for us to live an uncompromised life? Explain these verses on integrity.

Isaiah 45:23 _____

Isaiah 59:4 _____

Matthew 22:16 _____

Mark 12:14 _____

Titus 2:7 _____

21. God compensates his servants. Read and tell how He does this in 2 Corinthians 6:14-18, 7:1. _____

_____

_____

22. True or False: Godliness is always on purpose and profitable for now and eternity.   T   F

23. Give examples from your life experiences to support your answer.

_____

_____

_____

24. Have you resolved to remain faithful to Christ?   **YES   NO**

25. Is there anyone or anything that would tempt you to renounce your faith? _____

_____

26. In what areas of your life do you have victory by refusing to compromise? _____

_____

27. The rock represents what _____ and the kingdom will be _____.

When Government Goes Bad

We have no business to limit God's revelation

to the bias of the human mind.

Oswald Chambers

(The Complete Works of Oswald Chambers)

God is always about the unusual. He used a donkey to rebuke Balaam, the money-loving prophet. God sent a raven to feed the hungry prophet Elijah. It was God who woke up a rooster to broadcast the backsliding of the disciple Peter. It was God who warned a prideful King Saul with the bleating of sheep. Then, God troubled the sleep of King Xerxes until he found Mordecai's name in the historical chronicles. In Daniel 2, God sent a dream to trouble King Nebuchadnezzar. God is always about the strange and the supernatural.

The themes and prophecies exploding from the pages of the book of Daniel are about so much more than individuals. If Daniel, in his captivity, had thought that his life and assignments were all about him, he would have been miserable with the circumstances of his new existence.

Chapters 1-6 were originally written in Aramaic, indicating the message was for the Gentile people and not the Jews. Beginning in chapter 7, the language changed to Hebrew, signifying the rest of the book was intended for the Jewish people.

The King's Dream and Threat • Daniel 2:1-24

Nebuchadnezzar was trouble to God's people and now God would be trouble to King Nebuchadnezzar. A frightening and ter-

rifying dream made him restless. He knew the dream was important, more than just the product of a troubled subconscious
mind. His spirit was in turmoil and the imagery would not go
away. God has revealed much in dreams throughout the Old
Testament.

Pharaoh dreamed of the fat and lean cattle which were later
interpreted by Joseph. Jacob's vision of the ladder was a foreshadowing of Christ. Young Joseph saw himself in dreams ruling over
his brothers.

The King sent for all the magicians, sorcerers, astrologers and
enchanters in his kingdom to not only interpret the dream but to
also tell him what was in the dream. Either this was a severe test
of their authenticity or the King could not remember the dream
itself but was still troubled. He threatened these "wise" men with
dismemberment, death and the ultimate disgrace in a pagan
society, no burial if they failed.

All were shocked and dumbfounded at the King's preposter-
ous request. Their response was "only the gods whose dwelling is
not with flesh" could reveal such secrets. These pagan spiritualists
understood they were unable to solve the great riddles of the universe that were reserved for the supernatural. This truth is
revealed in John 1:14 which says, "The Word became flesh and
dwelt among us, and we beheld His glory, the glory as of the only
begotten of the Father, full of grace and truth." God alone knows
all.

In Daniel 2:12-13, the sentence of death was pronounced on
them and on Daniel and his friends. Daniel then appealed with
tact and directness to Arioch, the commander of the King's
guards, to ask for time to seek God on this matter. All the others
had given up. Not so with Daniel, for he knew the true and living
God and appealed to Him. God had Nebuchadnezzar's attention

and God had Daniel's appeal. The King knew dreams and visions came from the gods but he was about to learn that dreams are given by the only true God-Jehovah.

We, like Daniel, know that in a crisis we should not resist but always "resort" to prayer. Daniel had a personal history of prayer to count on and Daniel had knowledge of God answering prayer throughout the Jewish record of history. A few examples of times in scripture when God moved mightily through prayer include:

• In national crisis from 2 Chronicles 14:11-12
• In religious crisis in Acts 4:23-31
• In domestic crisis from Acts 9:36-43
• In personal crisis from James 5:13-14

Daniel called a Prayer Meeting

Daniel and his three Hebrew friends began to pray and ask God for mercy. These prayers were urgent as they pled their cause. They asked, they begged and they were probably on their knees and crying out loud. Daniel and his friends poured out their anguish to a holy God. Daniel had dear friends with whom he could pray about anything. Do you have good Christian friends you can pray with and trust with your deepest thoughts and concerns?

I imagine there was no sleep that night, for life and death hung in the balance. They trusted that God would give the answer to someone! When your life is on the line, can you trust someone's relationship with God to the point that your life depends on it? Hanaiah, Mishael, Azariah and Daniel had to trust God and each other.

There have been times when I have had to trust my husband's decision from God when I had not heard from God myself. That can be very disconcerting. These Hebrew young men were already labeled as wise men of Babylon and what a time to be in that group. That is one clique the young Hebrew men wanted out of immediately. Either God would answer with the dream and its interpretation or these four Hebrews would die with the other wise men of Babylon. All answered prayer is by the mercies of God. We receive answers not on who we are or what we are but through the mercies and goodness and grace of almighty God. In Daniel 2:19, God revealed the king's dream and its interpretation in a night vision to Daniel. I can only imagine the excitement they felt when they realized that God had come through for them and they would not die. Daniel blessed the Lord. They probably laughed, cried, sang, jumped, danced and shouted that Jehovah is holy and mighty. In verses 20-23, Daniel and his friends expressed thanksgiving and praise, for God had done exactly what they asked in prayer.

The test was over, the victory was won and the battle was complete. Their serious prayers revealed more secrets, and all ended in more praise to God and that is exactly what Daniel did when the answer came. In verses 20-23 he blessed God, shouted, danced, cried and praised God, who is sovereign over all. Daniel did not forget to say thank you to God. These four men worshipped God.

The proper order for placing a need before God includes prayer, then divine ministry, then worship. Even prayer is not worship and ministry is not worship. Prayer is asking of God and ministry is God giving something to man. When man has asked and God has given, then the heart is full and overflowing in adoration for God and this is worship.

The Dream and Its Interpretation • Verses 31 and 45

When Daniel was called to the king, Arioh tried to take some of the credit for the interpretation but Daniel was humble. Instead, Daniel glorified God and gave all the glory to Him. He made it clear that the dream was prophetic and it was revealing what would happen in the latter days. It was a panoramic view of the Gentiles for at least 2500 years, concluding with the second coming of Christ. Daniel also disclaimed any wisdom of his own in this matter. James 1:17 states that, "every good and perfect gift is from above, and comes down from the father of lights."

The King's dream covered a period known as "the times of the Gentiles." In Luke 21:24 Jesus called this era when the world was dominated by non-Jewish leadership, "...the times of the Gentiles." The times include the Babylonian captivity and continue until Christ comes again.

The great statue in the King's dream was composed of different metals creating the singular image of a man. The image was excellent and terrible at the same time. It was excellent to those who profited from it and terrible to those who didn't. The statue pictured a world, beginning with the days of Nebuchadnezzar and stretching forward in time to the millennium. (See page 50)

The Head of Gold is the Babylonian Empire

Babylon stood at the top of the Gentile world from 606-538 B.C. Babylon is called the golden city. Isaiah 14:3 says, "It shall come to pass in the day the Lord gives you rest from your sorrow, and from your fear and the hard bondage in which you were made to serve," and Jeremiah 51:7 proves this.

The Arms and Chest of Silver is the Medo-Persian Empire • Verse 39

Babylon would fall in one night to the Medo-Persian Empire. Two silver arms made up the two parts of this kingdom. The Medes and the Persians demanded taxes be paid in silver and they hid vast sums of silver. This empire lasted from 538- 331 B.C. and was inferior to the Babylonian Empire. Nebuchadnezzar's word was absolute because he was an absolute ruler - a despot.

The Medes and Persians ruled by law and they themselves were subject to the law. This was a kingdom divided between two countries and two leaders. See Daniel 6.

Silver is heavier and weighs more than gold but it is not as valuable. Since the gold section of the statue represents Babylon and the silver section, the Medes and Persians, the implication is that the Medes and the Persians ruled an empire inferior to Babylon. The type of metal in each section of the statue refers to the power, influence and importance of each empire to come which decreases with each world power.

The Belly of Bronze is the Greek Empire

This empire lasted from 331 B.C. to 169 B.C. Its greatest ruler was Alexander the Great, son of Phillip of Macedon. When Alexander came to Jerusalem the prophecy of Daniel was read to him. Alexander respected the prophecy. That is why the Greeks, under Alexander the Great, spared Jerusalem and the Jewish people. Greece was the empire of bronze. Their soldiers wore armor of brass and used swords of brass. See Daniel 8:21.

Alexander commanded that he himself be called the "king of the entire world." The two thighs in the statue were like the Medes and Persians, a combination of two adjacent countries –Greece and Macedonia. It is reported that Alexander the Great wept at the young age of 30 for there were no more worlds to conquer. Alexander the Great died at 33 years of age from complications of alcoholism and was buried with hands open and outstretched to show that nothing goes to the after life with a body. He left no heirs.

The Legs of Iron represent the Roman Empire
Verse 40

From 168B.C. to 476 A.D. the Roman Empire dominated the world. It is interesting that the armies of Rome were called the "iron legions". The divided Rome lasted until 1433 A.D. when the Turks defeated them at Constantinople.

Luke 2:1 says, "and it came to pass in those days that a decree went out from Caesar Augustus that the entire world should be registered."

Our Lord Jesus Christ was born at the time of the Roman Empire. This Roman Empire was in control while the Apostle John was on the Isle of Patmos writing the book of Revelation. Thus, the entire New Testament was written during the Roman Empire.

Under the Caesars, this empire conquered the known world. As each kingdom diminished in value, it increased in strength. The moral and personal values of each successive generation diminished. All of these kingdoms hungered for power and would do whatever it took to be the foremost power of the world.

The world has been in awe of Rome throughout the centuries. The founding fathers of the United States of America modeled our Senate after the Roman pattern of government. We use the symbol of the eagle as did Rome.

The Caesars were imitated by Germany with their Kaisers and Russians with their Czars.

The modern calendar follows the Roman dates. July is actually named for Julius Caesar, August for Augustus and October for Octavius Caesar.

The Feet and Toes are a mixture of Iron and Clay
Verses 41-43

The length of time between verse 40 and 41 is unknown. The legs of iron are the Romans but the vision goes to the final state of that kingdom prior to the second coming of Christ. The feet and toes were part iron and part clay. The rise and reconstruction of the Roman Empire in the last days will happen. Today we live with the influence of the Romans in law, religion, art, architecture, government, language, medicine and literature. No kingdom "put down" the Roman Empire, it dissolved at the hands of barbarians.

What we see in the statue is deterioration in stability as the image is top heavy in value and goes from gold to clay. It dissolves in disunity as the clay and iron refuse to blend and will not hold together. We see a deterioration of purity as two incohesive elements are put together. The kingdoms of this world are indeed shaky at best. Read in your Bible Revelation 17:10-12 and find these 8 kingdoms God has ordained throughout human history.
1. The Egyptian Empire
2. The Assyrian Empire

3. The Babylonian Empire
4. The Medo-Persian Empire
5. The Grecian Empire
6. The Roman Empire
7. The Revived Roman Empire (Now being prepared with ten horns and ten toes).
8. The Reign of the false Christ over the revived Roman Empire. Continue to reference this in Daniel 2:44-45, Revelation 19:11 and 2 Thessalonians 1.

Christ is the Stone that grows into the Mountain

He will be a holy place; for both Israel and Judah he will be a stone that causes people to stumble and a rock that makes them fall. And for the people of Jerusalem he will be a trap and a snare.
- Isaiah 8:14 (NIV)

For Jesus is the one referred to in the Scriptures, where it says, 'The stone that you builders rejected has now become the cornerstone.'
- Acts 4:11 (NLT)

The stone smites the image not on the head as one would suppose and not on the body or legs, but on the feet and toes. Christ will cause that imposing Colossus to crash to pieces.

Seven times in scripture our Lord is called a stone. Christ is the stone here in this dream. He came in the form of a servant and became a stone of stumbling to the nation of Israel. Israel fell on this stone and was broken in Matthew 21:44.

Anyone who falls on this stone will be broken to pieces; any-
one on whom it falls will be crushed.
- Matthew 21:44

Christ is the rock upon which the church is built and no other foundation must ANY man lay than Christ Jesus. Christ is the stone who is to fall on this stately image of man and grind it to powder.

(34) While you were watching, a rock was cut out, but not by
human hands. It struck the statue on its feet of iron and clay
and smashed them.
(35) Then the iron, the clay, the bronze, the silver and the gold
were all broken to pieces and became like chaff on a thresh-
ing floor in the summer. The wind swept them away without
leaving a trace. But the rock that struck the statue became a
huge mountain and filled the whole earth.
- Daniel 2:34-35 (NIV)

Nothing was left of the statue but the stone. The King of Kings and Lord of Lords, the cornerstone, remained. Christ is the stone that shall descend and fill the earth. To him be glory and honor and praise for He shall reign forever and ever. Our prayer is that His kingdom come and will be done on earth as it is in heaven.

The stone became a mountain and the 10 kings were crushed by heaven. In Joshua 8:30-31, Joshua and the Jewish men built an altar on Mt. Ebal. They were required by law to use whole, uncut stones to make the altar of sacrifice.

Jesus Christ will literally return for a 1,000 year reign here on earth. He has paid the price for our redemption and bought us back into a right relationship with God. Jesus Christ is the stone the builders rejected, meaning the one the Jews rejected. However, in the last days, the Jews will accept Jesus as the cornerstone.

In Psalm 118 we are reminded that on the eve of Christ's death our Lord ate the Passover meal with His disciples. In verse 22 Jesus told them He was the stone the builders rejected and the builder is Israel, but some day Israel will discover their cornerstone or capstone is the Lord Jesus Himself, the Passover Lamb. In Psalm 118:24, "This is the day the Lord has made, let us rejoice and be glad in it." We must be glad in this crucifixion day for it is ordained of God for man's salvation.

All four kingdoms, Babylonian, Medo-Persian, Greek and Roman, came to pass and then passed away in history. History has recorded that these kingdoms existed in the past and will reform just as Daniel's interpretation from God revealed.

The dream was for the future. The prophecy has already been fulfilled in history. What Daniel saw as prophecy, we now study as history. The word eschatology is the study of last, final and ultimate things in the end of days. This lesson in chapter two is both prophetic and eschatological. The dream covers Nebuchadnezzar's reign until the reign of Messiah. Luke 21:5 gives the signs of the end of the age. One of the signs is that they will be trampled by the Gentiles until the days of the Gentiles be fulfilled and these were all Gentile nations.

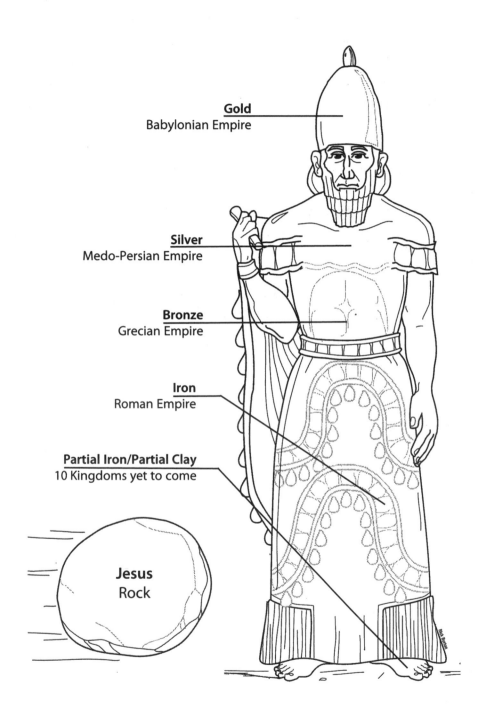

Gold
Babylonian Empire

Silver
Medo-Persian Empire

Bronze
Grecian Empire

Iron
Roman Empire

Partial Iron/Partial Clay
10 Kingdoms yet to come

Jesus
Rock

Study Guide

CHAPTER TWO • WHEN GOVERNMENT GOES BAD

Introduction

The second chapter of Daniel contains one of the most amazing prophecies of the Bible. It is a mountain peak of prophecy – very complete, yet a simple picture of the development and fall of world powers. What was a prophecy in Daniel's time is a study of history for us. God is declaring Himself and the future of His people on earth. The King's dream was a chronology of world history for the Gentile nations.

We, like Daniel, in a crisis should not "resist" but always "resort" to prayer. Reflect on God answering your prayers concerning.
"National Crisis" – 2 Chronicles 14:11-12
"Religious Crisis" – Acts 4:23-31
"Domestic Crisis" – Acts 9:36-43
"Personal Crisis" – James 5:13-14

1. Explain how God answered Daniel and his friends' prayers with: A definite answer (verse 19). What was it? _____

_____

_____

2. A miraculous answer (verse 19). Explain secret things. _____

_____

3. A humbling answer in a vision. Explain. _____

_____

4. Daniel prayed what prayer for the wise men of Babylon in verse 24? _____

5. What was the effect upon King Nebuchadnezzar? _____

_____

6. What rewards were given by the King to Daniel? _____

_____

The King's striking language refers to the Holy Trinity.
    God of Gods – God the Father
    Lord of Kings – The Son
    Revealer of Secrets – The Holy Spirit

7. Give examples from scripture of God doing the unusual. _____

_____

8. What has He done which was supernatural in your life recently?

_____

_____

Let's review why Daniel wrote the book in two languages.

9. What part is in Aramaic and why? _____
_____

10. What part is in Hebrew and why? _____
_____

11. How was King Nebuchadnezzar affected by his dream? _____
_____

12. Have you had troublesome dreams from God? Have they been interpreted for you? Explain:_____
_____
_____
_____

13. What strange demands did the King make on his magicians concerning the dream? _____

14. When Daniel was confronted with the King's command, what did he do? _____

15. Do you have friends to whom you can go with deep heart-felt prayers?   **YES   NO**

Review a time when your friends prayed you through to victory.

16. What did Daniel do when he received the interpretation and the dream from God? _____
_____
_____

Fill in the blanks regarding the meaning of the statue.

17. The head is made of _____ and represents the ruler _____. This represents the historical period of 626-539 B.C. _____. The chest and arms are made of _____. Daniel 2:39 refers to the _____ Kingdom from 539-331B.C. A famous ruler of that period was _____ (Isaiah 44:24). The belly and thigh are made of _____ (verses 32 & 39) and represent the ruler _____ from the empire of _____. The legs are of _____ (verses 33 and 40) and the kingdom is _____ 63 B.C. – A. D. 476. _____ was a famous ruler from this kingdom. The feet are made of _____ and _____ (verses 33, 41-43). The ten toes represent _____ that will operate at the time of Christ's return.

Chapter Three
Faith for Fiery Trials

My goal is God Himself, not joy, nor peace.
Not even blessing, but Himself, my God.
It is His to lead me there, not mine, but His –
"At any cost, dear Lord, by any road."

One thing I know, I cannot tell Him no;
One thing I do, I press toward my Lord;
My God my glory here, from day to day,
And in the glory there my Great Reward

Francis Brook b.1870

A truly happy person is one who can enjoy
the scenery while on a detour.
- Author Unknown

To this point in our study, do you think Daniel may have felt
that his life was on a detour? Yet, he seemed content. Let's look at
Daniel chapter three.

*(1) King Nebuchadnezzar made an image of gold, sixty cubits
high and six cubits wide,[a] and set it up on the plain of Dura
in the province of Babylon.*
*(2) He then summoned the satraps, prefects, governors,
advisers, treasurers, judges, magistrates and all the other
provincial officials to come to the dedication of the image he
had set up.*
*(3) So the satraps, prefects, governors, advisers, treasurers,
judges, magistrates and all the other provincial officials
assembled for the dedication of the image that King
Nebuchadnezzar had set up, and they stood before it.*
*(4) Then the herald loudly proclaimed, "Nations and peoples
of every language, this is what you are commanded to do:*
(5) As soon as you hear the sound of the horn, flute, zither,

lyre, harp, pipe and all kinds of music, you must fall down and
worship the image of gold that King Nebuchadnezzar has set
up.
(6) Whoever does not fall down and worship will immediate-
ly be thrown into a blazing furnace.
- Daniel 3:1-6

We don't know how much time had elapsed between chapter two and three, but let's guess at least 7 years. This is when Nebuchadnezzar decided that if he was the head of the statue in the dream, then he would just build an entire image of himself since nothing that Daniel saw had happened yet.

From building up our self-image, to manufacturing an over-sized image of a company through a marketing strategy, we know all too well about image building in our modern day "Babylon". The word image means to draw a likeness, to describe or reflect or picture in your mind. So an image could be:

• a mental representation
• a public image
• a popular image
• an altruistic image
• a professional image, hard-hitting, demanding and
  unscrupulous
• who you know
• what you know
• what you have
• what you wear and how you look

You can hire an image consultant to enhance your career but you will pay an image consultant $75 - $100 an hour. What kind of personal image do we portray? Most of us want to build our best image for others to see.

In Daniel 3:1-6 the King is had an image of himself built and declared himself a god. He made not only the head, as the prophecy had foretold, but the entire statue of gold. He wanted to unify Babylon and satisfy his power lust. He tried to do what they originally wanted in the Tower of Babel, which was discussed in chapter 1. This was not God's plan.

- In Genesis 1:26 the Holy Word says "let us make man in our image."
- I Corinthians 11:7 states, "Since man is the image and the glory of God."
- Colossians 1:15 says, "He is the image of the invisible God, the firstborn over all creation."
- Revelation 14:9 says "If anyone worships the beast and his image and receives the mark on his forehead..."
- Romans 8:29 "For whom he foreknew he predestined to be conformed to the image of His Son that he might be the first born among many."

It is not our image that is important. We are created in the image of God and it is the standard and image of the Holy God that we represent.

Testing before the Fiery Trial

The King made the statue 90 feet tall and 9 feet wide and set it in the circular plain of Dura. (The scripture uses the term "cubit" which is the approximate distance from the elbow to the tip of your middle finger, 18 inches.) It could have been made of pure gold and not just overlaid gold. He was self consumed and spared no expense for his image to be worshipped.

When the instruments played, everyone was to bow down and worship before this enormous image. No option! If they refused, a fiery furnace awaited them. This despot ruled through intimidation.

Remember in Daniel 2:46-49 that Daniel was promoted into leadership over the entire province of Babylon and chief over all the wise men in Babylon. Daniel sat at the gate of the King. His Hebrew friends Hananiah, Mishael and Azariah were also in leadership presiding over the affairs of Babylon. They had titles, riches and good reputations. But down the ranks, other leaders were jealous that these foreign men were promoted, ruling over them. So they watched them carefully. When the music blared and the masses began to bow, the three Hebrews did not. They didn't have to think about it or have a discussion. They were not tempted to rationalize or compromise their convictions. Their faith couldn't be bought! It was unacceptable to bow before an image made of hands. Contrary to public opinion, every man does not have a price! The three Hebrews did not bend and did not bow.

Sometimes, you are out there on your own. In this story Daniel, their leader, was not mentioned. We don't really know where he was but he does not appear in this story. Sometimes your pastor is not around. Your prayer partner is not available and your mentor is on vacation. Your life group leader isn't answering his phone! You are alone and it is your turn to step up in a difficult situation. These three young men were framed, so they had to man up. They didn't mince words, and there was no attempt to make peace with the furious king. Without hesitation they said, "We will not serve nor worship the golden image."

They knew Exodus 20:3-5. "You shall have no other gods before Me. You shall not make for yourself a carved image-any likeness of anything that is in heaven above, or that is in the earth beneath, or that is in the water under the earth. You shall not bow down to them nor serve them. For I, the Lord your God am a jealous God, visiting the iniquity of the fathers upon the children to the third and fourth generations of those who hate Me."

Isn't it amazing that while idolatry had led Judah into captivity, that idolatry offered these believing Jews an opportunity to take a stand for Yahweh-Jehovah God? They were tested, charged, arraigned, convicted, preserved and honored. They had strong spiritual backbones and stood tall for God.

Charged Before the King • Verses 8-12

The envious Chaldeans vented their jealousy to the King, reporting that Hananiah, Mishael and Azariah, the three Jews he had set over the affairs of Babylon, had violated his commands. I am sure they positioned themselves to gain the promotion that had been given to the Jewish aliens. They made three charges against them. First, that they had no respect for the King (untrue). Second, they did not serve the King's gods (true). And third, they did not worship the King's image (true).

Arraigned • Verses 13-18

When they were brought in before him, Nebuchadnezzar personally asked the men if they had disobeyed his command or misunderstood it. He had recently promoted them so he offered a second chance. They didn't even budge. They believed in the power of God to deliver them. They believed in the will of God. They would not worship other gods - no matter what happened. They held to the same conviction as many others in scripture.

• Job said, "though he slay me, I will trust him."
• Habakkuk praised God even in his suffering.
• The apostles rejoiced to suffer in His Name (Acts 5). James was martyred but Paul was released.
• Bishop Polycarp praised and glorified God while burning at the stake.

They had no need to defend themselves. They simply told the King, "If we are thrown into the blazing furnace, the God we serve is able to deliver us from it, and he will deliver us from Your Majesty's hand. But even if he does not, we want you to know, Your Majesty, that we will not serve your gods or worship the image of gold you have set up." (Daniel 3:17-18)

Then the fury of the king took over. The three Hebrews saw three possible options for themselves.

Delivered From the Fire

They believed they could be delivered FROM the fire. What a difference a preposition makes. Paul asked three times to be delivered from a thorn and affliction, but God answered and said, "My grace is sufficient."

I think of my dad who struggled with leukemia for 16 years. He sat through treatments at the cancer center which took 8 hours to administer every 28 days. We all prayed for a miracle. "God, let the cancer stop! Let it go away! Let it be an incorrect diagnosis." Our faith was strong; yet, dad was not delivered from the fire.

We prayed for God to remove the whole thing and I am sure that is what the three Hebrew young men prayed as well. "But if you do not choose to deliver, we will not bend, nor bow to any stone image."

Delivered Through the Fire

The second option was deliver THROUGH the fire. Going back to the cancer illustration, the test was complete and the news was "live with it". My dad went through chemotherapy and lived with the rare kind of leukemia and its limitation to his body. God did not take it away and did not cure my father, but God gave him 16 years of moderate strength and health. God had given life and it was still very good. Then what? We fought the cancer with everything in us and all we know of modern medicine

Our prayer was, "God deliver us through this fire and pain." In John 11:4 Jesus said, "This sickness is not unto death, but for the glory of God." The Hebrew men were truly being refined by fire.

Delivered By Fire

My dad was about to be delivered BY FIRE to our Savior's arms in death. We persevere in prayer and then we go to heaven. After 16 years living with this dark cloud of an illness, my father was diagnosed with lung cancer and given 6 months to live. No other option was open to us! We called in Hospice and determined to live every day to the fullest. The sadness was oppressive and the conversation hollow. My dad had 3 very good months of strength and joy. How he enjoyed sitting outside in the warm sunshine and how he marveled at the setting sun each evening.

Most of us want to stay here on earth because this is all we know. If we knew what heaven is really like, we would want it and want it now. "To die is gain," said Paul. We won't know that personally until it is our time to go. When it came time to say goodbye, my dad simply slipped into a coma. All six children and mates gathered around his hospital bed. A few grandchildren and two ministers were also there. After each one had whispered something in his ear, we sang "Jesus Loves Me". Just before he was delivered from his diseased body, he opened his crystal blue eyes, turned his head toward heaven and he was transported to glory . I know where my dad is and I know he will meet me there when it is my time to go because he promised he would!

For the three Hebrews, whether they were rescued from the fire, had to walk through the fire or were consumed by the fire, whatever the result, they would not bend or bow.

Sentenced • Verses 19-23

Infuriated over their defiance, the King lost his temper completely. He shouted to stoke the fire 7 times hotter and throw them in immediately, fully dressed in outer garments, sashes and turbans. Bound in ropes, they were thrown into the fiery grave. The King's burning anger resulted in the deaths of his own treasured hero soldiers who succumbed to his irrational decision to overheat the kiln he was preparing for the Hebrews. With arms and ankles bound, verse 23 says, "they fell down shackled in the fire".

Preserved unharmed • Verses 24-27

The King was astonished by what he saw.

> *(24) Then King Nebuchadnezzar leaped to his feet in amazement and asked his advisers, "Weren't there three men that we tied up and threw into the fire?" They replied, "Certainly, Your Majesty."*
> *(25) He said, "Look! I see four men walking around in the fire, unbound and unharmed, and the fourth looks like a son of the gods."*

Hananiah, Mishael and Azariah were thrown into the fire bound with ropes but soon were loose, and walking around in the flames unharmed.

The very thing that could have destroyed them resulted in their freedom. Romans 5:3-5 tells us that the sufferings in this life produce perseverance, character and hope, and that hope is poured into us by the Holy Spirit.

The fourth man in the fire was the pre-incarnate Christ–the second person of the Godhead. This type of appearance is called a Christophany, a physical appearance of Christ in the Old Testament before He was born, or in the New Testament after he ascended to heaven. He is Emmanuel, God with us. They were not alone. The Lord Jesus was with them.

Jesus came down from heaven and appeared to Adam and Eve. He walked with Enoch, instructed Noah, feasted with Abraham, wrestled with Jacob and spoke to Moses. He guided and provided for Israel through the wilderness. Then came to earth as a baby born in Bethlehem, God in the flesh, crucified for our sins and resurrected from the dead.

(1) But now, thus says the Lord, who created you, O Jacob. And He who formed you, O Israel: Fear not, for I have redeemed you; I have called you by your name; you are Mine. (2) When you pass through the waters, I will be with you; and through the rivers, they shall not overflow you. When you walk through the fire, you shall not be burned, nor shall the flame scorch you.
(3a) For I am the Lord your God . . .
- Isaiah 43: 1-3a

Remember dear friend, when walking through your own hot burning trials, you are not alone. The Hebrews were walking in the fire; not running or writhing in pain. They simply kept moving. For the Hebrews, the only thing that burned was the ropes that bound their hands and feet. We can be encouraged today. Tribulation fires will burn off the bonds or ropes that hold those who love Christ.

A very important fact to note is that Nebuchadnezzar, a pagan, recognized the fourth man in the fire was God. Wow! The pre-incarnate Christ showed up for the three young men of faith. The King admitted defeat but was amazed. The passage indicates that the face of the furnace was open so they could see in and that he shouted in and told them to come out. See Daniel 3:26-27. It's interesting that the furnace was open but they didn't leave the fire until they were told to. They stayed in the fire and communed with the Father until they were told to come out by the King.

Honored

Back in verse 15 the King used contemptuous words, "And who is that God that shall deliver you out of my hands?" But now he commended the Jews for their total commitment to Jehovah and issued a decree that nothing erroneous be said about the Judean God because there was no other god who was able to deliver in this way. Nebuchadnezzar recognized that the God of the Jews was a higher god than his gods but he did not become a believer in the God of Abraham at this point.

You can remain true to God even in the worst time of severe trials. Moral and spiritual compromise is NOT necessary. The courageous stand of Hananiah, Mishael and Azariah continues to be an Inspiration to the people of God everywhere who are walking through difficulty.

Study Guide

CHAPTER THREE • FAITH FOR FIERY TRIALS

Introduction

In Daniel 2:47 King Nebuchadnezzar made a confession that the God of the Hebrews was the God of gods. Unfortunately, the confession was temporary. The Babylonian age was pre-eminently the golden age of human history. Here the King made an image of priceless gold – probably intended by Satan to make Daniel's interpretation about the Empire's deterioration and destruction a lie.

By building the Tower of Babel, Nimrod was the first to attempt to unify the religions of man by self deification. In this passage Nebuchadnezzar attempts the same thing.

1. What were the two reasons why the image of gold was erected?

_____ represents

_____.

_____ represents

_____.

2. How much time had elapsed between Chapters 2 & 3? _____

3. The statue vision of Chapter 2 and the King's statue of Chapter 3 were different in what way? _____

_____

4. How tall was the King's statue and when was it set up?

_____

5. What was the requirement of the people regarding this monumental statue? _____

_____

6. Where is Daniel during this chapter? _____

7. Who were the Hebrews that refused to obey the King's command and what do their names represent in Hebrew and Aramaic?

Names   Meaning

_____   _____

_____   _____

_____   _____

8. Read and paraphrase these passages:

I Corinthians 11:7 _____

_____

_____

Colossians 1:15 _____

_____

_____

Revelation 14:9 _____

_____

_____

Romans 8:29 _____

_____

_____

Exodus 20:3-5 _____

_____

_____

9. If these men had been tempted to bow before the statue, what might have been some of their temptations? _____

_____

10. Read Isaiah 43:1-20 and write out the portion that could have given courage to these young men. _____

_____

11. Did they know that they had received a Divine Mandate - a set up to step up for God?   **YES   NO**

12. What were their options in a fiery furnace? What might their God do?

1. Deliver them _____ the fire.

2. Deliver them _____ the fire.

3. Deliver them _____ the fire.

13. Apply these options to your own fiery trials. For example, if cancer is found in your body, that is a fiery trial! What might God do?

_____

_____

14. In Daniel 3:17 what declaration did the three Hebrews make?

_____

_____

15. Read and paraphrase:

1 Peter 1:6-7 _____

_____

_____

Hebrews 12:1-2 _____

_____

_____

James 1:12 _____

_____

_____

1 Peter 4:11 _____

_____

_____

1 Corinthians 10:13 _____

_____

_____

16. What happened in the furnace? _____

_____

17. Who was the fourth man in the fire? _____

18. The Lord's presence and sweet fellowship was there in the fire. Notice the pre-incarnate Christ's presence with other biblical characters:

He came down and _____ with Adam and Eve.

He came down and _____ with Enoch.

He came down and _____ with Noah.

Examples of God manifested in the flesh as the second person of Godhead–Jesus:

He came down and _____ with Abraham.

He came down and _____ with Jacob.

He came down and _____ to Moses.

He came down and _____ Israel through wilderness.

He came down and _____ the tabernacle with His glory.

He came down as Virgin Mary's _____,

born in _____, _____ for our sins

and _____ from the dead.

He came down and _____ us through His Holy Spirit.

My friends, we are never alone in our fiery trials. Our Lord is not sitting or running but walking in the fire with us. He allows the fire to burn off bonds and ropes that are flammable. Our tribulation fires will free us from bondage and our chains will be gone.

When it's over, we won't smell like fire; we have full deliverance. Our clothes are not scorched and our hair is not singed.

Victory and deliverance in our fiery trials make our God famous!

What happened to the Hebrew boys immediately after the furnace experience?

Yeah, God! Tell someone about your own "yeah, God" experiences.

The scripture says, "Whom he foreknew he predestined to be in the image of His Son." In America, like Babylon, society is absorbed with image building – what we wear, how we talk, how we are perceived, who we know, and what we have, but God's Word says the Holy Spirit is our image builder – and that is to conform to the image of Jesus.

In the beginning of the chapter, Nebuchadnezzar had asked, "Who is that God that shall deliver you out of my hands?" He found out the answer after the miracle as he exclaimed: "There is no other God that can deliver."

Trials bring us closer to God. Read Hebrews 12:5-11, Romans 5:3-5 and Matthew 25:21.

Chapter Four
Finding God
When You Have Lost Your Mind

Bless the Lord Oh My Soul
Bless the Lord Oh My Soul
And all that is within Me,
Bless His Holy Name

Psalm 103:1

We have all had embarrassing or humiliating experiences but few of us are willing to share the details or make it a matter of public record. However, in Chapter 4 of Daniel, King Nebuchadnezzar issued a letter to his kingdom describing the most embarrassing and humbling circumstances of his life which I believe led to the his conversion. The chronological events in this chapter include: the warning to a prideful king, a year of unrepentance, God's judgment for his failure, and the King's restoration to the throne.

This is the last biographical section on King Nebuchadnezzar recorded in the book of Daniel and may have covered the end of his 43 year reign. The city of Babylon was complete and included the Hanging Gardens for his wife from Media and more than 50 temples built to honor various pagan gods. He was a great visionary and had built the greatest city and empire of the ancient times. King Nebuchadnezzar proudly took credit for it all.

With every construction project completed, the King sat back and marveled at the work of HIS hands, HIS accomplishments and HIS kingdom which deserved HIS acclaim and HIS worship. This King was a military genius who had defeated Egypt in 606 B.C. at the Battle of Carchemish and Judah in 605 B.C. He was a great statesman and administrator as the entire kingdom was prosperous and content under his egocentric leadership. The passage below reveals how God seeks to turn the heathen, the pagan, and a self-absorbed King from his wickedness.

(14) For God may speak in one way, or in another,
Yet man does not perceive it.
(15) In a dream, in a vision of the night, when deep sleep falls upon men, while slumbering on their beds,
(16) then He opens the ears of men, and seals their instruction.
(17) In order to turn man from his deed, and conceal pride from man.
- Job 33:14-17

This was not the first time God tried to get Nebuchadnezzar's attention. The first time God spoke to the King was in Daniel 2 when he dreamed of the great statue with the head of gold which represented King Nebuchadnezzar in his power and influence. The second time God spoke to the King was in the deliverance of Hananiah, Mishael and Azariah from the fiery furnace. Finally, in Daniel 4, God speaks to the king through a second dream. Before reading the dream, look at verses 1-3.

(1) King Nebuchadnezzar, to the nations and peoples of every language, who live in all the earth: May you prosper greatly!
(2) It is my pleasure to tell you about the miraculous signs and wonders that the Most High God has performed for me.
(3) How great are his signs, how mighty his wonders! His kingdom is an eternal kingdom; his dominion endures from generation to generation.
- Daniel 4:1-3

This introduction could easily be the conclusion to the chapter. The King wrote this letter to his whole kingdom to tell what God had done to and for him. He wanted everyone everywhere to know his testimony of how God humbled him and brought him low so he would learn to praise and worship the Most High God.

The King's Warning

(5) I saw a dream which made me afraid, and the thoughts on my bed and the visions of my head troubled me.
(6) Therefore I issued a decree to bring in all the wise men of Babylon before me, that they might make known to me the interpretation of the dream.
(7) Then the magicians, the astrologers, the Chaldeans, and the soothsayers came in, and I told them the dream; but they did not make known to me its interpretation.
(8) But at last Daniel came before me (his name is Belteshazzar, according to the name of my god; in him is the Spirit of the Holy God),
(9) and I told the dream before him, saying: "Belteshazzar, chief of the magicians, because I know that the Spirit of the Holy God is in you, and no secret troubles you, explain to me the visions of my dream that I have seen, and its interpretation.
(10) These were the visions of my head while on my bed:
I was looking, and behold, A tree in the midst of the earth, And its height was great.
(11) The tree grew and became strong; Its height reached to the heavens, And it could be seen to the ends of all the earth
(12) Its leaves were lovely, Its fruit abundant, And in it was

food for all. The beasts of the field found shade under it, the birds of the heavens dwelt in its branches, and all flesh was fed from it.

(13) I saw in the visions of my head while on my bed, and there was a watcher, a holy one, coming down from heaven.

(14) He cried aloud and said thus:'Chop down the tree and cut off its branches, strip off its leaves and scatter its fruit. Let the beasts get out from under it, and the birds from its branches.

(15) Nevertheless leave the stump and roots in the earth, bound with a band of iron and bronze, in the tender grass of the field. Let it be wet with the dew of heaven, and let him graze with the beasts' on the grass of the earth.

(16) Let his heart be changed from that of a man, let him be given the heart of a beast, and let seven times pass over him.

(17) 'This decision is by the decree of the watchers, and the sentence by the word of the holy ones, in order that the living may know that the Most High rules in the kingdom of men, gives it to whomever He will, and sets over it the lowest of men.'

- Daniel 4:5-17

This dream made the King greatly afraid. He had everything a person could want but peace, sleep, and security. In the dream he saw an enormous tree full of fruit, birds and nests with great shade for animals situated in a green meadow. Its height was great and its leaves were green. He saw watchers or holy ones (angels) coming down from heaven. He heard them say, "Chop down the tree and strip it of all leaves, fruit and birds. Scatter the animals far and wide from its shade but leave the stump and roots in the earth. Put a band of iron and bronze on the stump."

Suddenly the pronoun changes from "it" to "he". The rest of the dream foretells that he will be as an animal wet with dew and grazing like an ox or cow with an animal's heart for seven seasons. His hair will cover his body like that of an eagle and his fingernails will grow thick and long like the claws of a bird. How unnerving for the King!!

When all the magicians and soothsayers had failed to interpret the dream, the King called Daniel because he knew "the Spirit of the Holy God" was in Daniel and that no mystery was too difficult for him to unravel. (vs.9)

When Daniel heard the dream, he was immediately sorrowful for he knew the tree was the King himself. He was so stunned that he did not speak for a long time. Observing his troubled countenance, the King told him to speak truthfully and not be afraid to give the interpretation. With a sorrowful heart, Daniel related that the tree was King Nebuchadnezzar and that he would be cut down from his throne, removed from his kingdom, and lose his sanity. He would have a mental illness (possibly zoanthropy) which means he would think he was an animal and take on the behavior of a beast of the field.

Daniel's Words

Therefore, Your Majesty, be pleased to accept my advice: Renounce your sins by doing what is right, and your wickedness by being kind to the oppressed. It may be that then your prosperity will continue."
- Daniel 4:27 (NIV)

In verse 27 Daniel advised the King to repent of his sins, be righteous and show mercy to the poor in hopes that God would remove this judgment. However, this advice fell on deaf ears. King Nebuchadnezzar ignored Daniel and his advice. He forgot he was but dust. He refused to be accountable to the only true God. He refused to believe that he wasn't in charge; he was not supreme. He continued to glorify himself and his own great Babylon.

Pride is a sense of one's value and dignity. The sin of pride is an overly exalted opinion of one's self. An exalted sin of pride contrasts with the things of God.

One would think Nebuchadnezzar might be content in his position of authority but pride is never satisfied. Pride seeks more and more. The more we give in to pride – the more it wants.

The scripture has much to say about pride.

- *For the sin of their mouth and words of their lips, let them be taken in their pride. - Psalm 59:12*
- *When pride comes then disgrace but with humility wisdom. - Proverbs 11:2*
- *A man's pride brings him low but a man of lowly spirit gains honor. - Proverbs 29:23*
- *The pride of your heart has deceived you. You who dwell in the clefts of the rock, whose habitation is high. You who say in your heart, who will bring me down to the ground? Though you ascend as high as eagles. And though you set your nest among the stars. From there I will bring you down says the Lord. - Obadiah 2:3-4*

The scripture teaches that pride goes before a fall. We know from 1 Peter 5:5 that God resists the proud but gives grace to the humble. Ultimately, the King's pride caused his humiliation. Nebuchadnezzar ignored his own pride, but God did not ignore it. God gave the King one year to repent. Grace always comes before judgment. Man can think that he is all powerful, but God alone is in charge of us all.

Author Victor Hugo tells the story of Napoleon on the day of the Battle of Waterloo. Napoleon bragged, "At the end of this day, England will be at the feet of France." His senior officer replied, "But sir, we must remember that man proposes but God disposes." With anger and arrogance Napoleon boasted, "I want you to understand that Napoleon proposes, and Napoleon disposes." Hugo said, "From that moment Waterloo was lost, for God sent rain and hail and on that night it was Napoleon who was the prisoner of Wellington and France was at the feet of England."

Human pride brings a troubled life and King Nebuchadnezzar was about to find that out. His pride and his power ended in a sudden mental illness. Not all mental illness is judgment from God. But in this case his situation is the result of His actions – a judgment on the King.

The Wrath of Heaven

(29) At the end of the twelve months he was walking about the royal palace of Babylon.
(30) The king spoke, saying, "Is not this great Babylon, that I have built for a royal dwelling by my mighty power and for the honor of my majesty?"
(31) While the word was still in the king's mouth, a voice fell from heaven: "King Nebuchadnezzar, to you it is spoken: the kingdom has departed from you!
(32) And they shall drive you from men, and your dwelling shall be with the beasts of the field. They shall make you eat

grass like oxen; and seven times shall pass over you, until you know that the Most High rules in the kingdom of men, and gives it to whomever He chooses."
(33) That very hour the word was fulfilled concerning Nebuchadnezzar; he was driven from men and ate grass like oxen; his body was wet with the dew of heaven till his hair had grown like eagles' feathers and his nails like birds' claws.
- Daniel 4:29-33

Exactly one year later, the King was walking about his palace one night marveling and bragging to himself about all that he had done and what he had accomplished when he heard a voice from heaven saying that the kingdom had departed from him.

Instantly, he ripped off his clothes, lumbered on all fours, bellowed like a wounded bull and galloped from the palace to a field. All normalcy was gone. His rationality had left him. He became an insane, raving maniac, devoid of speech or communication.

God gets our attention one way or another. The watcher angels dispensed judgment quickly. God gives and God takes away. The King's hair grew long and coarse like eagle's feathers. His fingernails were long, hardened and thick like claws. He was mentally deranged but right where God had put him. As spoken in the dream, for the next seven years he lived like this. His swollen ego was gone. He was the tree chopped down but the stump was in tact and bound with iron. This means the stump would not split and the tree would be restored and grow again. Restoration was going to happen. There was a way back.

History records the lapse of years of the king's rule. Nebuchadnezzar is associated with the fall of a tree. Since he had transgressed the commands and warnings of God, he was coming under the judgment and chastisement of Almighty Jehovah for his pride. The way of the transgressor is hard. In the scripture the fall of man is associated with the tree in the Garden of Eden. Our salvation is associated with another tree called Calvary. The Bible says that the righteous are like a tree planted by the rivers of water. (Psalm 1:3) The fruit of the righteous is a tree of life. (Proverbs 11:30) Isaiah 65:22 states "like the days of a tree are the days of my people." Jeremiah says in 17:7 that "He (the righteous) is like a tree planted by water who sends out roots by the stream."

There is also a prophetic warning here. In the last days the Gentile world will be chopped down and there will be seven years where the antichrist rules and he is called the beast. It is no surprise that God would choose this for Nebuchadnezzar's dream. For seven years Nebuchadnezzar lived as an animal or beast totally devoid of human reasoning.

The King's Awakening

(34) And at the end of the time I, Nebuchadnezzar, lifted my eyes to heaven, and my understanding returned to me; and I blessed the Most High and praised and honored Him who lives forever:
For His dominion is an everlasting dominion, and His kingdom is from generation to generation.
(35) All the inhabitants of the earth are reputed as nothing; He does according to His will in the army of heaven and among the inhabitants of the earth. No one can restrain His hand or say to Him, "What have You done?"
(36) At the same time my reason returned to me, and for the glory of my kingdom, my honor and splendor returned to me.

My counselors and nobles resorted to me, I was restored to my kingdom, and excellent majesty was added to me.
(37) Now I, Nebuchadnezzar, praise and extol and honor the King of heaven, all of whose works are truth, and His ways justice. And those who walk in pride He is able to put down.
- Daniel 4:34-37

The King lifted his eyes to heaven. His understanding returned to him when he silently acknowledged the sovereignty, power and dominion of the Most High God. He blessed, praised and honored God. Nebuchadnezzar worshipped the King of Heaven and no other god from this point forward.

He had robbed God of honor and Nebuchadnezzar was robbed of his reason. When he looked up to honor God, it was God who restored his reason. The king was thankful to the Most High. He praised the living sovereign God as the omnipotent, righteous and holy, one true God. Elohim, Adonai and Yahweh are his names.

Was Nebuchadnezzar really converted? A resounding yes! The King realized the great lengths God had gone to get his attention, spare his life and bring him to faith in the God of Daniel. God brought an end to his humiliation. Free from bondage, he preached God's goodness. Can you say with Nebuchadnezzar that it was worth it? Look what the Lord has done for me!

He healed my body.
He touched my mind.
He saved me, just in time!

God went to great extremes to save this King, and rest assured that He does that for us, too. God answers, delivers, saves, restores and gives back abundantly.

The account of Nebuchadnezzar's journey to faith in the Lord is inscribed in Daniel so others may read it and receive God fully. It is pitiful that some people sink to the lowest level of maladies and degradation but never welcome the Most High into their lives.

He also wrote his message so that those who walk in pride will lay it down and avoid the humiliation of being brought down. The way up is down and the way down is up.

Look at the six times in this chapter that God is called the MOST HIGH God.

- Verse 2 – Signs and wonders that the Most High God has worked for me.
- Verse 17 – The Most High God rules in the kingdoms of men.
- Verse 24 – This is the decree of the Most High God which has come upon you.
- Verse 25 – Seven times pass over you until you know the Most High God rules in the kingdoms of men.
- Verse 32 – Seven times pass over you until you know the Most High rules in the kingdom of men, and gives it to whomever He chooses.
- Verse 34 – I blessed the Most High and praised and honored Him who lives forever.

The opposite of pride is humility and the way we achieve humility is by being humiliated. In our self sufficient me-focused society, we are headed for a fall like this king if we don't humble ourselves before the Most High God and repent of our sins. We are who we are and what we are because of the grace of God. Remove yourself from the "I am" mentality of Babylon and focus on the great I AM the one true and living God.

Study  Guide

CHAPTER FOUR
FINDING GOD WHEN YOU HAVE LOST YOUR MIND

Introduction

Daniel 4 records God speaking for a second time in a dream to King Nebuchadnezzar. The first dream was a great statue (Daniel 2). God also spoke through the excellence of Daniel and his friends in chapter one and through their delivery from the fiery furnace of chapter three. The King in chapter four reverts to his own pride, arrogance and self-sufficiency. In this chapter, God uses drastic circumstances to bring this prideful king to the end of himself and to faith in the God of Israel.

The climax of God dealing with this king brings embarrassment and humiliation. The King, in a letter to his people, makes this incident a matter of public record. This account is an example of the scripture in Job 33:14-17.

1. Explain King Nebuchadnezzar's dream. _____

_____

_____

_____

_____

_____

2. What was the interpretation of the dream by Daniel? _____

_____

_____

_____

_____

_____

3. How was this dream fulfilled? _____

_____

_____

4. This is not about mental illness but divine discipline. Those who walk in pride, God is able to _____.
The way up is down.

5. Paraphrase 1 Peter 5:5 _____

_____

_____

_____

_____

6. List and explain the two previous warnings from God to Nebuchadnezzar.

    A. _____

    _____

    B. _____

    _____

7. What was the warning of the "tree" dream? _____

_____

_____

8. How long a time did God give the King to repent? _____

_____

_____

This chapter adds to our understanding about angels.
9. What are "watcher" angels (verse 23)? _____

_____

Read:
• Hebrews 2:1-3   • 2 Peter 2:4
• Revelation 12:3, 4   • 1 Peter 1:12

10. What does the fettered (chained) stump illustrate? _____

_____

_____

11. How do you know Nebuchadnezzar became a believer?
Explain. _____

_____

_____

_____

12. Why did God use a "tree" as the symbol for man? _____

_____

13. The fall of man relates to what tree? _____

14. The salvation of man relate to what tree? _____

15. Explain the symbol in the following verses:

Psalm 1:3 _____

_____

Proverbs 11:30 _____

_____

Isaiah 65:22 _____

_____

Jeremiah 17:7 _____

_____

16. Security, contentment and prosperity were important to Nebuchadnezzar. How important is each one in your life? Explain. _____

_____

_____

17. What is real living in your opinion? _____

_____

_____

It boils down to an abundance of things or an abundance of God.

18. Look at Daniel 4:19-27, 32, 34 and write down six occasions for the title "Most High".

A. _____

B. _____

C. _____

D. _____

E. _____

F. _____

19. Some things don't need to be cut back; they need to be cut off. Name someone or something that needs to be deleted from your life. We must break off some friendships or these friendships will break our testimony and possibly our morals. _____

_____

_____

20. How was Nebuchadnezzar's dream fulfilled? _____

_____

_____

21. His mental illness lasted how long? _____

_____

22. What intervention changed Nebuchadnezzar forever? _____

_____

_____

_____

_____

_____

Chapter Five
Dead Man Walking

But in a great house there are not only vessels
of gold and silver, but also of wood and clay,
some for honor and some for dishonor.

Therefore if anyone cleanses himself from the latter,
he will be a vessel for honor, sanctified and useful
for the Master, prepared for every good work."

2 Timothy 2:20-21

History records that while the city of Rome burned to the ground, the emperor Nero played his fiddle. In much the same way, King Belshazzar threw an enormous feast for one thousand of his lords, wives and concubines, which also included dancing and a drunken orgy, while the Medes and Persians were entering the foremost city of the world. We have often heard people sing of God's unseen hand but here the seen hand of God appears and puts an end to a man and a kingdom within an hour.

As chapter 5 opens, it has been 23 years since Nebuchadnezzar died and approximately 30 years have elapsed between chapters 4 and 5. Four different people have taken the throne during that time, the result of rebellion and murder. After the death of Nebuchadnezzar, his only son, the evil Merodach, ruled briefly. He was murdered by Negaglasser (Nergal-Sharezer) Nebuchadnezzar's son-in-law. This evil king was succeeded by his young son, Labashi-Marduk, who ruled only two months and was murdered by Nabonidus, another son-in-law to Nebuchadnezzar. Nabonidus ruled 17 years with his son, Belshazzar, as co-regent. This is fulfillment of Jeremiah 27:6-7 which lists the generations of Nebuchadnezzar. Belshazzar was the grandson of Nebuchadnezzar. Nabonidus, who advanced the kingdom with his constant military campaigns,commanded the army in different parts of the world. Belshazzar ruled within the city and provinces. Notice that there is no Hebrew word for grandson or great grandson. That is why Mephibosheth is called the son of Saul and Obed is called the son of Naomi. We are all called sons of Abraham or sons of Adam.

The History of Sins

(1) Belshazzar the king made a great feast for a thousand of his lords, and drank wine in the presence of the thousand.

(2) While he tasted the wine, Belshazzar gave the command to bring the gold and silver vessels which his father Nebuchadnezzar had taken from the temple which had been in Jerusalem, that the king and his lords, his wives, and his concubines might drink from them.

(3) Then they brought the gold vessels that had been taken from the temple of the house of God which had been in Jerusalem; and the king and his lords, his wives, and his concubines drank from them.

(4) They drank wine, and praised the gods of gold and silver, bronze and iron, wood and stone.

(5) In the same hour the fingers of a man's hand appeared and wrote opposite the lampstand on the plaster of the wall of the king's palace; and the king saw the part of the hand that wrote.

(6) Then the king's countenance changed, and his thoughts troubled him, so that the joints of his hips were loosened and his knees knocked against each other.

- Daniel 5: 1-6

The Medo-Persian armies had already begun the conquest under the army general Cyrus but Belshazzar, who should have protected his people, was resting in self-assurance and boasting of his pleasures, power and security. He was a pleasure seeker who feasted and hosted great parties even when the enemy was at the gates. He acted as though he had no worries and a good time was more important to him than the defense of Babylon. He should have been fasting before God but instead he feasted and drank a LOT of wine.

For 3 months the Persians had surrounded the city, yet they still celebrated. They believed they were safe because the walls were 87 feet thick and 350 feet high for 60 miles in a perfect square with 250 watchtowers which were 100 feet higher than the walls. The city was well fortified but no wall, tower or gate could hold back the hand of God's judgment.

Belshazzar was host to an outrageous party of revelry, debauchery, lust, and drunkenness. It was an unprecedented breach of culture to invite women to participate with men but here he includes the wives and mistresses of the leadership of Babylon. If he could get them drunk enough, they would have the same inflated false sense of security as Belshazzar. After all, he had accumulated a supply of food for the city that would last for 20 years. It was protected by double walls and watchtowers, and a continuous supply of water flowed from the Euphrates. Belshazzar did not know he was a condemned man and this would be his last party.

Belshazzar's Final Sin

In the midst of his drunken feast he committed blasphemy by letting his guests drink from the holy vessels of the Temple of God which had been taken as spoils of war from Jerusalem.

Why were these vessels special?

A review of their history will explain. First of all, let's look at Daniel 1:2. "And the Lord gave Jehoiakim king of Judah into his hand, with some of the articles of the house of God, which he carried into the land of Shinar to the house of his god; and he brought the articles into the treasure house of his god. These were the holy vessels taken out of the Temple in Jerusalem and placed in the temple of his god, Bel."

In verse 2 it was Adonai (Hebrew for Lord) who allowed the people to be taken captive and Adonai who allowed the holy vessels to be stolen. So for 50 years King Nebuchadnezzar had the Holy goblets stored in his treasure house.

Look at Leviticus 8:10-11 which says; "Also Moses took the anointing oil, and anointed the tabernacle and all that was in it and consecrated them. He sprinkled some of it on the altar seven times, anointed the altar and all its utensils, and the laver and its base, to consecrate them."

Every article and item in the tabernacle was anointed. The Hebrew word for anointed is Masiyah which is our Messiah - The Anointed One.

In 2 Chronicles 7:16, God says of Solomon's Temple, "For now I have chosen and sanctified this house that My name may be there forever; and My eyes and My heart will be there perpetually." The Temple was anointed, pure, set apart and holy to God.

People and things are often set aside and reserved exclusively for God. Yet, King Belshazzar, in a drunken stupor, took these precious anointed holy goblets and toasted their gods of gold, silver, bronze, iron, wood, and stone and drank from God's consecrated vessels. Just notice in this passage that the king in verse 2 asked for the vessels of gold and silver but in verse 3 they only brought the vessels of gold. Could that be because this was the gold kingdom, the gold head on the statue we learned about in chapter 2? The Babylonian Empire represented by the gold head of the statue in chapter 2 is about to fall with a crash. The Medes and Persians, who are represented by the silver arms of the statue, are about to take over suddenly.

Believers are also holy vessels before the Lord as stated in 2 Timothy 2:20-21 and Ephesians 1:1. Paul addresses the New Testament Christians as the saints in Ephesus – holy ones set apart because of salvation in Jesus Christ. We are indeed holy, sacred, separated and devoted to God. 2 Corinthians 1:21-22 says that God has anointed us and set His seal on us and our eternity is secure. There is no false security here. He has set His name on us.

Satan does not want you to know you are holy. He tries to desecrate what God consecrates just like Belshazzar did by his disgraceful use of the temple articles. When Belshazzar disrespected the God of the Hebrews with full knowledge of the history of Nebuchadnezzar, he fell under the judgment of God.

The book of Daniel is so relevant today. A nation is doomed when its leaders are weak and godless. How can a nation feast while it is under siege? How can a nation survive that overlooks indecency? What is going to happen to a nation that caters more to the Hollywood crowd than to ordinary citizens? Why are so many of the people of the United States uninformed about or not interested in the Bible and the powerful messages it contains, but actively seek out every kind of smut on bookshelves, on the internet and in the entertainment media?

Belshazzar mocked and abused that which belonged to God. Belshazzar disregarded history. (Verse 22) He knew the Almighty had dealt with his grandfather and revealed great and wonderful things to him. Today we live as though we are ignorant of God's hand on our lives and our nation. Our children do not read about Ben Franklin's call to prayer at the Constitutional Congress or know that George Washington bowed on his knees and prayed at Valley Forge. Do our children know it was Jonathan Edwards who called this nation to God, founded Harvard University and caused the Great Awakening to sweep over America? Oh, we need a Great Awakening again to avoid disaster.

The Death Certificate of a King

(4) With the sacred gold wine-filled goblet in hand, Belshazzar challenged the God of the Hebrews and God took the challenge.
(5) As they drank the wine, they praised the gods of gold and silver, of bronze, iron, wood and stone.
(6) Suddenly the fingers of a human hand appeared and wrote on the plaster of the wall, near the lampstand in the royal palace. The king watched the hand as it wrote. His face turned pale and he was so frightened that his knees knocked together and his legs gave way.
- Daniel 5:4-6 (NIV)

The unseen hand of God suddenly became the seen hand of God writing supernaturally on the plaster of the palace wall. When the King saw the writing, he was fearful, shaking, troubled, and according to verse 6, his face changed. Belshazzar's thoughts haunted him, joints in his hips loosened and his knees knocked together in fear.

There are many times in scripture when the finger of God related to man.

- Exodus 8:9 the finger of God brought the plagues on Egypt.
- Exodus 31:18 the finger of God wrote the law.
- Luke 11:20 the finger of God cast out devils.
- The finger of God wrote on the ground through the incarnate Christ and Pharisees left an adulterous woman alone.

Belshazzar was a drunken despot but now he is in total despair. The book of Proverbs gives wisdom about the foolish man and indeed Belshazzar was a very foolish man and king.

- *Pride and arrogance and the evil way and the perverse mouth I hate.* - Proverbs 8:13
- *He who hates, disguises it with his lips, and lays up deceit within himself.*   Proverbs 26:24
- *Do you see a man wise in his own eyes? There is more hope for a fool than for him.* - Proverbs 26:12
- *A fool's wrath is known at once.* - Proverbs 12:16
- *An evil man seeks only rebellion; Therefore a cruel messenger will be sent against him.* - Proverbs 17:11
- *A fool's mouth is his destruction, and his lips are the snare of his soul.* - Proverbs 18:7
- *Do you see a man hasty in his words? There is more hope for a fool than for him.* - Proverbs 29:20

Belshazzar was wicked to the core. He lived a life of personal consumption, desperate without God or guidance from the prophet Daniel. His life of dishonor, arrogance and corruption was full of destructive consequences that were about to be judged by almighty God.

Tragically, none of the court could read the writing. It seems that Daniel had not been active at court because Belshazzar did not know him.

(10) The queen, hearing the voices of the king and his nobles, came into the banquet hall. "O king, live forever!" she said. "Don't be alarmed! Don't look so pale!

(11) There is a man in your kingdom who has the spirit of the holy gods in him. In the time of your father he was found to have insight and intelligence and wisdom like that of the gods. King Nebuchadnezzar your father — your father the king, I say — appointed him chief of the magicians, enchanters, astrologers and diviners.

(12) This man Daniel, whom the king called Belteshazzar, was found to have a keen mind and knowledge and understanding, and also the ability to interpret dreams, explain riddles and solve difficult problems. Call for Daniel, and he will tell you what the writing means."
- Daniel 5:10-12 (NIV)

The queen (Nitocris) heard the anguished conversation of her son (Belshazzar),and entered the ballroom. She advised him in verse 10, to pull himself together, call Daniel and act like the king!

The Mystery

Daniel was over 80 years old and had no sympathy for Belshazzar as he once had for his grandfather. He brought three charges against the king.

- You sinned against the light of knowledge.
- You deliberately defiled God by desecrating the holy vessels.
- You worshipped idols (verse 23).

Daniel interpreted the writing as follows: "Mene" means numbered and "Your number is up." The days of Belshazzar's reign were numbered. "Tekel" means weighed. He was found too light to fulfill God's expected purpose as an earthly leader. He misused his position and privileges. "Upharsin" means broken as in "Your kingdom is broken up". The kingdom will be given to the Medes and Persians.

God raises up and God brings down. Judgment came upon Belshazzar swiftly. Following the supernatural prophecy and the interpretation by Daniel, the words were fulfilled before their eyes. On the very night the armies of the Medes and Persians were completing the diversion of the Euphrates River, the armies marched under the city walls on dry riverbeds. This well fortified and self sufficient empire crumbled in a single night. History records the exact date, October 12, 539 B.C. Everything went to the Medes and Persians.

You may look at this story and say, "That was then and this is now. It can't happen to me." But the warning here is for everyone. There is a last night, a last dance, a last fight, a last word, a last supper, a last call, a last movie, a last drink, and a last oath for everyone.

Darius the Mede was the Uncle of Cyrus and the commander of the army. The general who took possession of the city and killed Belshazzar was Gobryas. Ezra 6 records that about a year later Darius died and Cyrus came to the throne. Remember, this is the king who allowed 50,000 Hebrews to return to Judah and to rebuild their temple. He also gave them back the holy sacred vessels so the Hebrews could guard them carefully. God does not overlook the mistreatment of what He has set apart for himself. Likewise, he takes seriously the mistreatment of His children - His living holy vessels.

As I have stated in earlier chapters, we live in a Babylonian type culture today that teaches "it's all about me" and personal image is everything. Have you recognized this bombardment on your life personally?

How much will you weigh on God's set of scales? Belshazzar was a lightweight. We will not be weighed according to our club memberships, our bank accounts, social standing, church affiliation, education or accomplishments. We will be weighed on the scales of Almighty God.

All a man's ways seem innocent to him, but motives are weighed by the LORD.
- Proverbs 16:2.

The divine handwriting of justice has been written against all who are unsaved. Colossians 2 :14 states, "Having blotted out all handwriting on the wall that was against us, which was contrary to us, and he took it out of the way, having nailed it to the cross, having disarmed principalities and powers, He made a public spectacle of them, triumphing over them in it."

There was a time when my life stood condemned by what was written against me. But thanks to the victory of Jesus over sin at Calvary and death at the empty tomb, the condemnation against my life has been erased as it can be for everyone who will fall at the feet of Jesus in repentance.

Chronological Chart of Babylonian Rulers
Chapter 5 Appendix

626 B.C. . . . .**Nabopolassar, King of Babylon**
Overthrew Assyria
He died in 605 and his son ruled

605 B.C. . . . .**Nebuchadnezzar rises to power**
Ruled 43 years

562 B.C. . . . .**Death of Nebuchadnezzar**
Merodach's (fool) son

560 B.C. . . . .**Neriglassar ruled**
He was Merodach's brother-in-law
Assassinated Merodach in 560 B. C.
Jeremiah 39:3,13

556 B.C. . . . .**Nerigrassar's son Labashi-Marduk**
Ruled two months
Assassinated by Nabonidus

556 – 539 B.C. . . . .**Nabonidus**
Ruled 17 years
His son Belshazzar was co-regent

539 B.C. October 12 . . . .**Belshazzar's Banquet**
Handwriting on wall
Daniel was in his 80's when he interpreted the handwriting.
Both the King and Kingdom died that night.
The army marched into Babylon unhindered.

Outline of Attack on Babylon
(Cambridge Ancient History Records)
Chapter 5 Appendix

• Earlier King Astyages of Media defeated by his grandson,
  Cyrus II of Persia (Jeremiah 51:61)

• Cyrus mobilized army 539 B.C. and captured Opis (north of Babylon)

• He divided his army and he attacked Sippar and Gobryas marched
  unhindered to Babylon.

• Euphrates flowed through middle of Babylon.
  A large bridge connected the East to West.

• A tunnel existed under the river with numerous canals used to irrigate
  outside city.

• Persian army constructed dam some distance away rerouting
  Euphrates River around Babylon not through it.

• A distracted populace and relaxed military allowed armies to march in
  by night on these dry river beds under gates of the city.

Babylon
Chapter 5 Appendix

- Babylon geographical place/city (Iraq), 60 miles South of Bagdad on Euphrates, present town Al Hillah.
- Babylon's religious system abhorrent to God – Revelation 17
- Babylon's political system Gentile – world system since Nimrod – Genesis 10:10 - Second Coming – Revelation 19:19-21
- Sumerians first inhabitants
- Descendent Nimrod and Cush – First noted ruler, Hammerurabi, 1728-1686 B.C. (under later Hittites, Kassites, Elamites
- Sennarerib Assyrian 689 B.C.
- Chaldean Empire united with Nabopolassar in 625 B.C.
- Babylon became capital city
- Under Nebuchadnezzar II (son of Nabopolassar) it became most glamorous city of known world.
- King Nebuchadnezzar made wide streets, canals, temples, palaces, Ishtar Gate and Hanging Garden
- October 13, 539 B.C. fell to Cyrus Great (Persia)
- Later partially destroyed Xerxes I of Persia because of rebellion
- Alexander Great 331 B.C. captured it and tried to rebuild – cost was prohibitive
- 200 B.C. it fell to Parthian control
- 200 A.D. it fell to Sassanian rule. Crumbled to ruins, Sodom and Gomorrah represented moral depravity and political degeneration. Babylon represented abject apostasy and unbelief.

Who Is Darius the Mede?

Jeremiah 50 and 51 recount the fall of Babylon. Isaiah 45:1 confirms that Cyrus is the Lord's anointed.

- Chaldea fell to Medes and the Persians
- Army that captured Babylon under Persian general Gobryas under Cyrus
- The man assuming leadership was Darise a Mede (not the same person)
- Medes and Persians related by marriage which Mede King Astyages arranged.
- He married off his daughter, Mandane, to Camlyses, King of Anshan. Darius then had a son, Cyrus King of Persia.
- Astyages also had a son, Darius Cyaxares II, who is Darius Mede and uncle to Cyrus.
- Cyrus then married the daughter of Darius
- When Darius died, Cyrus took the title, King of Persia

Miscellaneous

- Nabonidus was left alive
- Daniel third ruler Kingdom
- Satraps – Greek word – Princes "guardian, keeper"
- 120 – in provinces – Daniel over them.

Study Guide

CHAPTER FIVE • DEAD MAN WALKING

Introduction:

Alexis de Tocqueville said that the secret of America's greatness was her goodness. When she ceases to be good, she ceases to be great. That truth also applied to Babylon. A strong nation must have strong moral leadership. King Belshazzar feasted while his nation was under siege by an enemy. He was lured by a sense of false security. He did not know that this was his last meal. God signed the death warrant of the nation and the death certificate of a man that night. Judgment must come to all who refuse to come to God.

1. Give a primary subject statement for each chapter.

Daniel 1 _____

_____

Daniel 2 _____

_____

Daniel 3 _____

_____

Daniel 4 _____

_____

2. Who is the new Babylonian ruler in Chapter 5? _____
_____

3. What is Daniel's Babylonian name? _____
Circle the letters in the spelling of the name that are different.

4. Belshazzar was a co-regent with his father _____
who was son of _____.
This fact explains why Belshazzar was able to offer to
_____ to be a third ruler of the Kingdom.

Read 1 Corinthians 1:18-25. Notice we are called sons of God's –
sons of Abraham – sons of Adam.

5. Mephibosheth was called son of _____

6. Obed was the son of _____

7. What supernatural feat interrupted the drunken party of the
King? _____
_____

8. How did Belshazzar respond when his magicians and sorcerers
couldn't read the message? Who recommended that Daniel be
called in? _____
_____

9. What did she say about Daniel?_____
_____

10. What was Belshazzar's chief mistake?_____

_____

_____

11. How was the nation destroyed in an hour?_____

_____

_____

12. How was Belshazzar killed?_____

_____

13. Have you personally experienced similar circumstances or chastisement by someone you love that scared you so bad you determined to avoid that? Explain without names. _____

_____

_____

_____

14. Rephrase 1 Peter 5:5. _____

_____

_____

_____

_____

_____

15. What 4 words did God write on the wall?

_____   _____

_____   _____

16. Explain how each word applies to Belshazzar (verse 26-28)

_____

_____

_____

_____

_____

Head of Gold is gone. Empire of Silver has arrived.

17. Describe the fortified city of Babylon.

_____   _____

_____   _____

_____   _____

19. Read Leviticus 8:10-11 and explain. _____

_____

_____

_____

19. What was Belshazzar's great mistake? _____

_____

_____

_____

20. Who conquered the nation? _____

21. How are we the sacred vessels or saints of God? _____

_____

_____

22. Do you see yourself as holy?   **Yes**   **No**
The scripture says you are.

23. How did the empire of gold end? _____

_____

24. The empire of silver is who? _____

25. Who is the leader of the empire of silver? _____

26. What did King Cyrus do for the Jewish people as recorded in
Ezra 6? _____

_____

27. Give specifics: _____

_____

_____

_____

_____

Fill in the Book of Daniel timeline.

28. 612 B.C. _____

_____

29. 605 B.C. _____

_____

30. 562 B.C. _____

_____

31. 560-556 B.C. _____

_____

32. 555-539 B.C. _____

_____

33. 539 B.C. _____

_____

34. 465-424 B.C. _____

_____

Chapter Six
Living with Lions

Faint not, nor fear, but go out to the storm
And to action, trusting in God whose
Commandment you faithfully follow.

Dietrich Bonhoeffer

C hapter 6 is the final chapter on the lifestyle of faith and biography of Daniel. Next to the birth of Jesus, the most familiar story in the Bible is probably the story of Daniel and the lions. Leadership has been passed to the Medes and Persians under King Darius. Again, Daniel has found favor with the regime, but like his ancestors, his faith will be tested.

Favor

(1) It pleased Darius to appoint 120 satraps to rule throughout the kingdom, with three administrators over them, one of whom was Daniel
(2) The satraps were made accountable to them so that the king might not suffer loss.
- Daniel 6:1-2

Daniel was probably around 82 years of age when he was promoted by the new king, Darius. The empire was divided into 120 provinces, with 3 presidents over the 120 satraps or princes. Remember before Belshazzar's death, he had made Daniel one of these three rulers over the kingdom alongside Nabonidus, Bleshazzar and Daniel – a political triumvirate. Darius then gave Daniel favor and power to help restructure the kingdom.

Now Daniel so distinguished himself among the administrators and the satraps by his exceptional qualities that the king planned to set him over the whole kingdom.
- Daniel 6:3

God put Daniel in this favored position in opposition to the cultural idea that senior citizens should retire and live quiet, unobtrusive lives. This aging, faithful senior citizen should have lived out his days in peace, but notice that in his old age, Daniel stood the tallest in his faith.

He had lived out the entire 70 years of captivity and would live until the third year of Cyrus's reign when 50,000 Jewish people would be allowed to return to Judah.

Framed • Daniel 6:7-8

Daniel was about to be promoted to second in command over the entire nation. The other Babylonian leaders were jealous that a foreign captive, and Semitic Hebrew, would rule over them in their own land. Jealousy often leads to antagonism and becomes mental murder of that person. These Mede and Persian leaders were grasping at straws to find a way to discredit Daniel and bring him down. The only way the others in leadership could attack Daniel was to attack his God. Throughout his captivity in Babylon, Daniel was loyal to his God and respectful of the leaders in authority and God promoted Daniel above all others.

The same principle is found in the New Testament parable of the master and his servants. In Matthew 25:21 the master tells his servant who has been diligent with his assignment, "Well done, good and faithful servant; you were faithful over a few things, I will make you ruler over many things. Enter into the joy of your Lord."

There are those who can always be found ready with incredible destruction using a malicious tongue! Those in this chapter were full of hate and sought Daniel's death with their schemes. The scripture has much to say about the malevolent actions of the other leaders.

- *A lying tongue hates those who are crushed by it and a flattering mouth works ruin.* - Proverbs 26:28
- *Though I redeemed them, Yet they have spoken lies against Me.* - Hosea 7:13(b)
- *I said in my haste, "All men are liars."* - Psalm 116:11
- *And the tongue is a fire, a world of iniquity. The tongue is so set among our members that it defiles the whole body, and sets on fire the course of nature; and it is set on fire by hell.* - James 3:6

The scripture also says to be sure that your sins will find you out. The plot from Daniel's enemies became clear much too late for the King to put an end to it.

(7) The royal administrators, prefects, satraps, advisers and governors have all agreed that the king should issue an edict and enforce the decree that anyone who prays to any god or man during the next thirty days, except to you, O king, shall be thrown into the lions' den.
(8) Now, O king, issue the decree and put it in writing so that it cannot be altered — in accordance with the laws of the Medes and Persians, which cannot be repealed.
(9) So King Darius put the decree in writing.
- Daniel 6:7-9 (NIV)

Some of the leaders approached King Darius, convincing him to sign a Royal Decree that for 30 days no one in the kingdom would have any religious freedom except to pray to or worship King Darius. Of course, the King was flattered and puffed up in pride to think that he was an object of worship and importance. So he willingly bought into this idea and signed the law. If anyone broke this law, the punishment was to be thrown in a den of lions. Of course, Daniel was not included in the creation of this Royal Decree. The other leaders had to act quickly to develop and execute their plan.

The accusers of Daniel were so jealous that they themselves were lions seeking to kill this one whom they were required to serve.

Lions can be found many times in the scripture. We know Israel marched under the banner of the lion and in Revelation 5:5, the Lord Jesus himself is called "the lion of the tribe of Judah." Psalm 22:13 speaks of the persecution of the Christ when it says, "They gape at me with their mouths, as raging lions." In 2 Timothy 4:17 when the Apostle Paul was delivered from his first appearance before Caesar, he said, "I was delivered from the mouth of the lion." In I Peter 5:8 our archenemy Satan is described as a "roaring lion seeking whom he may devour."

The King had listened to his subjects and signed the Royal Law. This kingdom was ruled differently than Nebuchadnezzar in that Darius ruled alongside his princes and he, too, was subject to the Royal Law. Darius was not an absolute ruler and when he signed the law with his signet ring, it was totally irrevocable. So the kingdom had no religious freedom for 30 days.

Faithful

Now when Daniel learned that the decree had been pub-
lished, he went home to his upstairs room where the win-
dows opened toward Jerusalem. Three times a day he got
down on his knees and prayed, giving thanks to his God, just
as he had done before.
- Daniel 6:10

Daniel did not let the threat of lions intimidate him–whether we are talking about the ferocious beasts or the human beings who were after him. What kept Daniel from fear was faith in his holy God of Israel. More than the life of an old prophet was at stake here–the reputation of Jehovah God was on the line. Daniel had shown that he was trustworthy and neither corrupt nor neg-ligent in his faith. His spiritual life was now illegal but he would not compromise. His prayers were against the law but he would not stop praying. He had obeyed the powers over him until they conflicted with serving the sovereign God. What is required of believers when the will of God conflicts with the laws of the state? The scripture says in Acts 5:29 to obey God rather than man. Daniel did not give a second thought to the punishment at hand.

Daniel might have prayed 2 Chronicles 7:14 which says, "If my people who are called by My name will humble themselves and pray and seek My face, and turn from their wicked ways, then I will hear from heaven, and will forgive their sin and heal their land." He prayed daily in his chamber by an open window facing the holy city, Jerusalem, longing for his people to return to their homeland. Daniel knew that prayer was a sacred responsibility and privilege. His habit was to kneel, showing a total surrender and helplessness. He folded his hands to show nothing could be done in his own power and when he shut his eyes, the world, and its pull was removed.

Some of Daniel's prayers could have been:

- *But you O God, shall bring them down to the pit of destruction. Bloodthirsty and deceitful men shall not live out half their days. But I will trust in you.* - Psalm 55:22
- *Delight yourself also in the Lord and He shall give you the desires of your heart. Commit your way to the Lord. Trust also in Him and He shall bring it to pass.* - Psalm 37:5
- *. . . and Eli said, "It is the Lord. Let Him do what seems good to him?"* I Samuel 3: 18b
- *Trust in the Lord with all thine heart and lean not to your own understanding. In all your ways acknowledge Him and He shall direct your paths.* - Proverbs 3:5-6
- *I will cry out to God Most High. To God who performs all things for me. He shall send from heaven and save me. He reproaches the one who would swallow me up. God shall send forth his mercy and his truth.* - Psalm 57: 2-3

The spying accusers stalked Daniel and when they discovered him praying, they reported immediately to the King. They demanded that very day that Daniel be thrown in the den of lions. All too late, the king realized that he had been tricked and manipulated.

Daniel 6:14 says that, "When the king heard this, he was greatly distressed; he was determined to rescue Daniel and made every effort until sundown to save him."

With no other recourse, that very evening the King commanded that Daniel be brought to the den of lions. The King spoke to Daniel saying, "Your God whom you serve continually, He will deliver you." Daniel was faithful to God even in the face of a horrible death. But Daniel had always believed God.

I think an interesting point here is that there was a deep place in the King's heart for Daniel. And even though the King had not come to embrace Jehovah at this point, Daniel's godly lifestyle and respectful nature was softening the heart of the King, who by his own admission believed that Daniel's God would deliver him from the lions. Our lives are being observed closely by the people around us. Our words and actions will either lead people closer to or farther away from a relationship with Christ.

In sharp contrast to the King's love for Daniel, the King James Version strongly emphasizes the contempt these other leaders had for him, describing him as "that Daniel" in verse 13, signifying that he was less than human, a despicable, unworthy slave.

Early in the evening Daniel was placed in the den and the opening was covered. The King's wax seal was placed on the opening along with the marks of all the accusers.

Can you imagine the darkness of that pit in the night? Daniel couldn't see the lions but he could smell them and perhaps hear them breathe, feeling their hot breath near him in the threatening night air. I would love to believe that Daniel slept peacefully using the back of a lion as a pillow, and was kept warm by the massive mane of the wild beast.

The King did not fare as well as Daniel. Verse 18 tells us that he "returned to his palace and spent the night without eating and without any entertainment being brought to him. And he could not sleep." His heart yearned for Daniel and considered him a loyal subject, trustworthy and honorable in all things.

He was troubled and grieving for this faithful and trusted subject. I am sure he paced back and forth and was angry with himself and Daniel's accusers.

Finally Free

(19) At the first light of dawn, the King got up and hurried to the lions' den.
(20) When he came near the den, he called to Daniel in an anguished voice, "Daniel, servant of the living God, has your God, whom you serve continually, been able to rescue you from the lions?"
- Daniel 6:19-20

Notice the distressed emotional state of the King. He was grieving and overcome with sorrow. But Daniel answered from the pit, "O King, live forever! My God sent His angel and shut the lions' mouths so that they have not hurt me, because I was found innocent before Him and also, O King, I have done no wrong before you." Daniel did not have a scratch on his body. Hallelujah!

Make no mistake, God still ruled Persia, and God showed up in answer to Daniel's prayers, sending an angel to shut the mouths of those lions. I have seen God shut the mouths of human lions who talked against His work. You can be confident that if God can send one angel to put to death 185,000 Assyrians, then a few lions are a small order for the Mighty One. (2 Chronicles 32:21; Isaiah 37:36) God rules, reigns and intervenes for believers. God was there with Daniel through it all.

The King was overjoyed and gave orders to lift Daniel out of the den.
- Daniel 6:23

Daniel was freed by King Darius and by the King of Kings. The character of Daniel was exemplary with integrity and consistency.

He had courage, faith and devotion to God. God delivered Daniel and will deliver us from the lions of adversity. Hebrews 11:6 reminds us without faith it is impossible to please God. God is a rewarder of those who diligently seek Him. Daniel calmly and quietly trusted God. He was delivered because he believed in God.

- In Hebrews 11:5 Enoch was translated to heaven because he believed God.
- In Hebrews 11:7 Noah built an ark because he believed God.
- In Hebrews 11:8 Abraham went out from Ur not knowing where because he believed God.
- In Hebrews 11:22 Joseph commanded his bones to be taken away from Egypt because he believed in God.
- Moses refused to be called the son of Pharaoh's daughter because he believed in God.
- In Daniel 6:32-33 Daniel saw the mouths of lions shut because he believed in God.

What could God do through your life if you had this kind of faith in God? Hundreds of years after Daniel's death, Bishop Polycarp, pastor of the church of Smyrna which is mentioned in Revelation 2, was facing martyrdom by fire. He could have escaped if he renounced his faith publicly. However, it is recorded in history that he said to the crowd just before being martyred, "86 years have I served Him and He never did me injury. How can I blaspheme my Lord and Savior?" Polycarp stepped into his eternal reward that day. Daniel, Polycarp and countless others throughout history have trusted God with their very lives and found Him faithful!

Final Farewell

Daniel's accusers learned painfully that you never hurt others without hurting yourself. Verse 24 states, "And the King gave the command and they brought those men who had accused Daniel, and they cast them into the den of lions-them, their children, and their wives; and the lions overpowered them, and broke all their bones in pieces before they ever came to the bottom of the den."

Be sure your sins will find you out. Nothing escapes the ever watching eye of the Lord. In an attempt to discredit the supernatural nature of this biblical account, critics have suggested that the lions did not eat Daniel because they were not hungry. The description of the violent deaths of Daniel's betrayers in verse 24 puts to rest that possibility. In fact they were ravenously hungry because the lions caught their victims in the air before they could hit the ground.

The accusers received their just reward. In ancient times entire families were killed in punishment for one member's sin so that there would not be a future uprising or attempt on the King's life by any descendents of those punished or executed.

Proverbs 26:7 states, "Whoever digs a pit will fall into it. And he who rolls a stone will have it roll back on him."

Proverbs 19:12 states, "The king's wrath is like the roaring of a lion, but his favor is like dew on the grass."

Remember that Nebuchadnezzar had come to believe in the God of Daniel because of his faithful life. Likewise Darius, in verses 25-27, wrote a proclamation to the whole kingdom extolling the God of Daniel. "He is the living God and steadfast forever. His kingdom is the one which shall not be destroyed and His dominion shall endure to the end." Did Darius become a believer of the one true God? I believe so.

Our God rules and reigns and gives supernatural signs and wonders. It is true the accusers were punished in the way that they wanted Daniel to die. The triumph of the wicked is short. It doesn't pay to hurt others. Jealousy is a vile sin.

Notice the testimony of Daniel's life in captivity. Also notice that Daniel was highly favored by God and rewarded by man.

Daniel . . .
Prayed..knelt 3 times daily
Praised ....gave thanks
Persistently sought God ....whom thou serves continually
Persecuted ....captive from Judah
Protected..shut lion's mouths
Persevered ....no harm, no wound
Preferred ....this Daniel
Prospered ....2nd in command

In verse 28, "this" Daniel prospered and was promoted. He received favor and advancement from the king. Our God comes through every time. Don't let the lions of this world scare, surprise or subvert you. We all face lions in our lives – lion sized problems or lion sized people, but our God is our deliverer from them all.

The true story is told concerning Dr. Charles Stanley when he first became pastor of First Baptist Church in Atlanta, Georgia many years ago. There were "lions" that tried desperately to oust him as their pastor. On one occasion he was struck in the face in the pulpit while the live broadcast went out to the city.

During a particularly low moment in the crisis, a dear elderly widow had Dr. Stanley over for lunch. After the meal, she showed him a picture of Daniel in the lion's den. She asked him repeatedly, "What do you see in that picture that is different?" Pastor

Stanley made several wrong attempts to answer her question. Finally with tears in her eyes, she said. "Don't you see dear Pastor, Daniel is not looking at the lion; he is looking upward to God." Then she said, "Look at the Lord, not the lions."

That is the true secret of living with lions.

Study Guide

CHAPTER SIX • LIVING WITH LIONS

Introduction

God had severed the head of gold from the image of Gentile world power. Now the silver arm of the Medes and Persians were on the scene. It was 538 B.C. and Daniel was in his eighties. Why couldn't this old soldier live out his days in peace? No, as the leader of leaders in the King's cabinet, he was always subject to attack. The scripture tells us that the enemy (Satan, that stealthy roaring lion) seeks to kill, steal and destroy. Daniel had faced down the luxury, lust, licentiousness and lions of his age. Again, God intervenes.

1. What happened to Belshazzar and his kingdom? _____

_____

_____

_____

2. How were the Medes and Persians able to enter Babylon and subdue it without war? _____

_____

_____

3. Read Jeremiah 25:11-12 and write how long he prophesied that the captivity would last._____

4. Read Jeremiah 29:10-14 and find out what would happen to the Jews after the completion of those years._____

_____

_____

5. What kind of place was Babylon? _____

_____

_____

6. Notice that the rulers were jealous of Daniel and they were anti-Semitic. How and why? _____

_____

_____

7. What were they jealous of and why did they hate Daniel?

_____

_____

8. What was the royal law signed by King Darius? _____

_____

_____

9. How did Daniel break that law? _____

_____

10. What was Daniel's punishment? _____

_____

11. Why could the King NOT change the law? _____

_____

12. What happened to Daniel in the lion's den? _____

_____

13. Did the King sleep that night? _____

14. Did Daniel sleep? _____

15. The entire kingdom said Daniel was delivered. Why? _____

_____

_____

Who else in scripture was delivered like Daniel and how?

16. Enoch _____

17. Noah _____

18. Moses _____

19. Joseph _____

20. How did Daniel react in an emergency? _____

21. How would you usually react in an emergency? _____

_____

A consistent lifestyle is our protection of our integrity. Read the following from Daniel and explain how he was victorious and lived a life of integrity before God.

- Daniel 2:22
- Daniel 2:47 is the King's response.
- Daniel 3 (the statue and the fiery furnace)
- Daniel 4 (interprets King's second dream)
- Daniel 4:35-37 explains the King's praise of God
- Daniel 5:23 is the interpretation of the finger writing on the palace wall.
- Daniel 6 – Daniel, now over 80 years old, is saved from the lion's den.

22. Explain: _____

_____

_____

_____

As in his youth, Daniel had unswerving loyalty to God. He lived an uncompromised life. Our Lord Jesus Christ set the example for an uncompromised life. Through consistent living, we too can achieve the freedom to soar if we resist compromise.

23. What kinds of things would Daniel have missed in these 6 chapters had he not been devoted to God? _____

_____

_____

Don't let the lions surprise you. Lions are prominent in the Bible. One of the emblems Israel marched under was the lion. When the enemy like a roaring lion seeks to kill, steal and destroy you, the "Lion of the tribe of Judah" (Revelation 5) will defend you with His strength and ferocity.

Remember how God delivered you from the lions and give Him praise. So, in the future, don't let the lions scare you. Keep your eyes on the Lord, not the lions.

24. There were some in this chapter who did NOT escape the lions. Explain. _____

_____

_____

25. How does this parallel with what happened to Haman in the book of Esther? _____

_____

_____

_____

_____

_____

Chapter Seven

The Coming World Leader

All hail the power of Jesus' name!
Let angels prostrate fall;
Bring forth the royal diadem
And crown Him Lord of all.

Ye chosen seed of Israel's race
Ye ransomed from the fall;
Hail Him who saves you by His grace,
And crown Him Lord of All.

O that with yonder sacred throng
We at His feet may fall
We'll join the everlasting song,
And crown Him Lord of all.

Edward Perronnet
Adapted by John Rippon

With this chapter we begin the second half of the book of Daniel. In this last half of the book, we find that the aged and venerable Daniel is not only interpreting dreams as he did in previous chapters, but now he is receiving visions from God himself with the interpretations regarding the future eschatological events.

In chapter 7, the vision came in the first year of Belshazzar. The second vision, in chapter 8, was given in the third year of the reign of Belshazzar. The third vision, in chapter 9, was given in the first year of the reign of King Darius and the next vision came in the third year of the reign of King Cyrus as revealed in chapter 10. The last vision, in chapters 11 and 12, came in the first year of Darius the Mede. Chapters 1-6 were basically historical while the remaining half was prophetic.

Daniel's visions spanned the events of the first and second coming of the Messiah and all the related judgments, but were pictured as happening close together. When we view majestic mountain peaks from a vast distance, we think we see peaks side by side. As we get closer, we observe that they may be hundreds of miles apart. This is also very true of the stars and planets in the heavens. On a brilliant summer night they may appear to be very near to each other, while in reality they are actually millions of miles apart.

This is true of the Old Testament prophets. As they look across the vast expanse of the future through the prophetic lens, all the great mountain peaks seem near to each other and the large valleys inbetween the peaks cannot be seen. Today, we live in a large valley between the first coming and the second coming of Christ.

When one of the great highway tunnels was built in Colorado, the work began simultaneously on opposite sides of the mountain. When the crews met in the middle they were only one-half inch off center. This was considered an engineering marvel. But the prophecies of the Bible are more accurate than that. They are absolutely dead on perfect. They never miss the mark. Be assured of that.

The Vision Received • Daniel 7:1-14

(1) In the first year of Belshazzar king of Babylon, Daniel had a dream and visions of his head while on his bed. Then he wrote down the dream, telling the main facts.

(2) Daniel spoke, saying, "I saw in my vision by night, and behold, the four winds of heaven were stirring up the Great Sea.

(3) And four great beasts came up from the sea, each different from the other.

(4) The first was like a lion, and had eagle's wings. I watched till its wings were plucked off; and it was lifted up from the earth and made to stand on two feet like a man, and a man's heart was given to it.

(5) And suddenly another beast, a second, like a bear. It was raised up on one side, and had three ribs in its mouth between its teeth. And they said thus to it: 'Arise, devour much flesh!'

(6) After this I looked, and there was another, like a leopard, which had on its back four wings of a bird. The beast also had four heads, and dominion was given to it.

(7) After this I saw in the night visions, and behold, a fourth beast, dreadful and terrible, exceedingly strong. It had huge iron teeth; it was devouring, breaking in pieces, and trampling the residue with its feet. It was different from all the beasts that were before it, and it had ten horns.

(8) I was considering the horns, and there was another horn, a little one, coming up among them, before whom three of the first horns were plucked out by the roots. And there, in this horn, were eyes like the eyes of a man, and a mouth speaking pompous words.

(9) I watched till thrones were put in place, and the Ancient of Days was seated; His garment was white as snow, and the hair of His head was like pure wool. His throne was a fiery flame, its wheels a burning fire;

(10) A fiery stream issued and came forth from before Him. A thousand thousands ministered to Him; ten thousand times ten thousand stood before Him. The court was seated, and the books were opened.

(11) I watched then because of the sound of the pompous words which the horn was speaking; I watched till the beast was slain, and its body destroyed and given to the burning flame.

(12) As for the rest of the beasts, they had their dominion taken away, yet their lives were prolonged for a season and a time.

(13) I was watching in the night visions, and behold, One like the Son of Man, coming with the clouds of heaven! He came to the Ancient of Days, and they brought Him near before Him.
(14) Then to Him was given dominion and glory and a kingdom, that all peoples, nations, and languages should serve Him. His dominion is an everlasting dominion, which shall not pass away, And His kingdom the one which shall not be destroyed.
- Daniel 7: 1-14

In most passages, the sea refers to the Mediterranean but here it refers to the nations - the masses, the mobs and the Gentiles. The winds speak of tornados from the four corners of the earth which represent agitation, propaganda, public opinion and great disturbances. From these waters four beastlike kingdoms and kings appear on the global stage. Remember the statue from Chapter 2; this is similar but greatly enlarged.

The first beast is a lion with eagle's wings. The wings were pulled off and it was left standing on two legs like a man and a human mind was given to it. This is symbolic of the Babylonian kingdom (612 B.C. to 539 B.C.). Its national symbol was a winged lion. The wings represent the swiftness of the conquests of this strong and cruel kingdom. This also calls to remembrance Nebuchadnezzar's insanity and his ultimate conversion when he changed and became more humane in his rule. When his sanity left him, it was as though the wings were pulled off.

The second beast is the bear in verse 5. It represents the Medo-Persian rule from 539-331 B.C. Even though these two nations were both strong, the Persians were more powerful than the Medes. The three ribs in their mouths were Babylon, Lydia, and Egypt who were subjugated under Darius. Yet, they were still hungry for power, so they continued their conquests all the way to the Aegean Sea.

The third beast was the leopard, symbolic of Greece and the conquests of Alexander the Great. Greece was foremost in power from 331-63 B.C. defeating Persia. The four wings represented unusual speed as Alexander lamented at just 30 years of age that there were no more worlds to conquer.

The four heads revealed the division of the empire at Alexander's death. Since he had no heirs, his kingdom was divided among his four generals. It was remarkable that an army of 35,000 conquered the world. But God willed it and allowed it to happen.

In verse 7 the fourth beast comes forth and it is complex and hideous beyond description. This terrible, dreadful, and very strong creature crushed and devoured its victims with its huge iron teeth and trampled what was left under its feet. This represents the Roman Empire whose symbol is iron. The fourth beast had 10 horns and another little horn appeared and destroyed three of the horns. It gained power and cast fear on all the others. Revelation 13:10 is a companion study to this passage. Rome's iron clad legions conquered the world and its influence lives on.

The final world kingdom will be a culmination of the cruel little horn mentioned here. When the barbaric hordes came in to destroy Rome, no other nations came together to set up a new government. Many small kingdoms throughout Europe were established and patterned after Roman rule.

So Daniel 7:8 is a prophecy of the coming world dictator who will rise out of the influence of the Roman Empire. Satan does not know God's timing or his plans, so he has had an Antichrist positioned for every generation.

Napoleon sought to re-establish the Roman Empire. Mussolini saw himself as a new Caesar. Hitler's third Reich was a revived Roman Empire. The former Shah of Iran spent millions to restore the ancient splendor of Rome.

• Antichrist in Daniel 7:8 is called the little horn
• Antichrist in Daniel 8:23 is called the king of a fierce countenance
• Antichrist in Daniel 9:26 is called the prince that shall come
• Antichrist in Revelation 6:2 rides on a white horse (imitating Christ)
• Antichrist in Revelation 13:1 is the beast out of the sea
• Antichrist in II Thessalonians 2:3 is the man of sin, the son of perdition
• Antichrist in II Thessalonians 2:8 is the wicked one
• Antichrist in I John 2:18 is the Antichrist

Notice the difference between Chapter 2 and Chapter 7. The statue in Chapter 2 is presented as a mighty metallic Colossus and in Chapter 7 four wild beasts. From man's viewpoint the statue, representing kingdoms, is the concentration of all material wealth, pomp and power. From God's viewpoint they are a set of wild, rapacious, bloodthirsty beasts, devouring and destroying one another.

This little horn of Daniel 7:8 is a prophecy of the coming world dictator. The scripture warns of Satan's son and last masterpiece who will hold the final world order under his sway.

This aged Daniel saw the coming of the Antichrist and the return of the Christ of God. This vision also includes an unholy trinity that imitates the triune God because Satan wanted to be God and have everything God had.

So Satan is the Dragon of Revelation. The Beast is the Antichrist, who tries to imitate the Christ. The False Prophet imitates the Holy Spirit. However, they are no match for the heavens because right at this point, verses 8-14, the vision shifts to a heavenly scene.

The Ancient of Days, God the Father, who is seated upon the throne gets ready to judge as He is the Chief Justice of the universe. Clothing worn by the Ancient of Days is "white as snow," symbolizing absolute moral purity (Is. 1:18 and Rev. 1:14). Holy angels appear in white also. His hair is white like wool. White hair is a sign of old age and a symbol of God's eternal nature. God is holy and because He is holy, He judges sin.

His throne is a fiery flame, its wheels are a burning fire. Fire is a symbol of judgment. A fiery stream issued from before him. This means the burning wrath of God is about to destroy the wicked. God's chariot-throne has wheels and goes where He desires. It is also detailed in Ezekiel 1 and 10. The roaring fire is judgment coming on the little horn and the beast when Christ returns. Daniel 7:10 tells us that a thousand thousands ministered to Holy God – in other words, an infinite number ministered and stood before the throne.

The books are the account of the wicked deeds of the Antichrist and his evil empire and when they are opened Antichrist is judged. Daniel not only sees this in a vision, he is part of the scene. He sees one like the Son of Man. And who was it who called himself the son of man? Our Lord Jesus Christ. Daniel sees Him come in the clouds of heaven to the Ancient of Days. There He is given dominion and a kingdom of all peoples, nations, and languages that will serve Him.

When the Son of Man approaches the Ancient of Days (human picture of the eternal God), the Father says to the Son,

"Ask of me, and I will make the nations your inheritance, the ends of the earth your possession," Psalm 2:8. So, the Son asks and Holy God delivers.

The Son will come to judge His foes, claim His inheritance and reign forever. See Revelation 11:15. "Then the seventh angel sounded: And there were loud voices in heaven, saying, "The Kingdoms of this world have become the kingdoms of our Lord and of his Christ, and He shall reign forever and ever." At the second coming of Christ, He will be crowned sovereign ruler of the world. This is also the stone attacking the feet of clay and iron from chapter 2.

The "Son of Man" is the head of restored humanity. The "Son of David" is his royalty, and the "Son of God" is his deity. The saints win and the Ancient of Days rules on our behalf.

Daniel was so confused by this vision that he asked one near him to explain what he was seeing.

Vision Interpreted • Verses 23-28

(23) Thus he said: 'The fourth beast shall be a fourth kingdom on earth, which shall be different from all other kingdoms, and shall devour the whole earth, trample it and break it in pieces.
(24) The ten horns are ten kings who shall arise from this kingdom. And another shall rise after them; He shall be different from the first ones, and shall subdue three kings.
(25) He shall speak pompous words against the Most High, shall persecute the saints of the Most High, and shall intend to change times and law. Then the saints shall be given into his hand for a time and times and half a time.

(26) 'But the court shall be seated, and they shall take away his dominion, to consume and destroy it forever.
(27) Then the kingdom and dominion, and the greatness of the kingdoms under the whole heaven, shall be given to the people, the saints of the Most High. His kingdom is an ever-lasting kingdom, and all dominions shall serve and obey Him.'
(28) This is the end of the account. As for me, Daniel, my thoughts greatly troubled me, and my countenance changed; but I kept the matter in my heart.
- Daniel 7: 23-28

The "little horn" has eyes with penetrating insight and discernment (v. 8). He has an imposing personality and is very attractive (v.20). His arrogant words blaspheme God, but are believable and persuasive (v.8). He has great authority and has eyes that see everything. This gives new meaning to the phrase, "big brother is watching!" He has legal control of the 10 kingdoms and the world. His great speaking ability has given him political control. Both his handsome and intelligent appeal has given him social control. Yet, he will hate the Jews and all who support them and he will hate the things of God. The Antichrist is the worst of the world powers. He proclaims himself to be God. Other names for this little horn are:

- Man of Sin - 2 Thessalonians 2:1-10
- Son of Perdition - 2 Thessalonians 2:3
- Beast - Revelation 13:1-8
- Antichrist - I John 2:18

This evil one speaks against God and persecutes and oppresses the tribulation saints in an attempt to destroy them. He manipulates, seduces and gets what he wants. He makes war with the tribulation saints, changes laws relating to ordinary affairs of government but also religion and worship. The period of time is 3.5 years, a time and times and a half time. A "time" equals one year. This is half the length of the 7 year tribulation.

The beast comes to a sudden and disastrous end in verses 26-27. He is consumed and destroyed forever and the establishment of God's glorious kingdom on earth takes place and the saints inherit it. This counterfeit king will be destroyed at Christ's coming and the true King and kingdom will be established.

This beast, which had the power of the world, that harassed, afflicted and even martyred many, is no more. This wicked one is consumed and destroyed forever. The establishment of God's glorious kingdom on earth takes place and the saints of God inherit the earth and win the war with the beast. The Ancient of Days rules on the believer's behalf. This is the beginning of the Millennial Reign of Christ on earth.

(11) Now I saw heaven opened, and behold, a white horse. And He who sat on him was called Faithful and True, and in righteousness He judges and makes war.

(12) His eyes were like a flame of fire, and on His head were many crowns. He had a name written that no one knew except Himself.

(13) He was clothed with a robe dipped in blood, and His name is called The Word of God.

(14) And the armies in heaven, clothed in fine linen, white and clean, followed Him on white horses.

(15) Now out of His mouth goes a sharp sword, that with it He should strike the nations. And He Himself will rule them with a rod of iron. He Himself treads the winepress of the fierceness and wrath of Almighty God.
(16) And He has on His robe and on His thigh a name written: king of Kings and Lord of Lords.
- Revelation 19: 11-16

The Lord Jesus Christ, called the Faithful and True in this passage, rides on a white horse to judge and to make war. His eyes are flames of fire. Remember the symbol of fire means judgment is coming. On the head of Christ are many crowns. When we sing Matthew Bridges' hymn, Crown Him with Many Crowns, we are singing scripture.

Crown Him with many crowns;
The Lamb upon His throne:
Hark! How the heavenly anthem drowns all music but its own
Awake My Soul and sing
Of Him who died for thee,
And hail Him as thy matchless King throughout eternity.

He is clothed in a robe dipped in blood and His name is the Word of God. "In the beginning was the word and the word was with God and the Word was God. He was in the beginning with God. All things were made through Him and without Him nothing was made that was made. In Him was life and the life was the light of men." John 1:1-4.

In Revelation the armies of heaven all ride on white horses accompaning the Son of God. Notice in verse 15 that out of His mouth is a sharp sword. He doesn't have to wield a sword or gun in battle, only His word is needed. As He speaks the word, the

Antichrist is defeated and all war ends. On his robe is written King of Kings and Lord of Lords.

In verses 20 and 21, the beast and the false prophet were cast alive into the lake of burning fire and brimstone. They were killed by the word proceeding out of the mouth of the Christ on the white horse. Revelation 11:15 states, "And there were loud voices in heaven saying, 'The Kingdoms of this world have become the kingdoms of our Lord and of his Christ and He shall reign forever and ever.'" Hallelujah! Worthy is the Lamb who was slain and Holy is He. Coronation takes place for the Messiah King.

At the headquarters of the United Nations in New York City, a portion from the Book of Isaiah is inscribed on a marble wall. "They shall beat their swords into plowshares, and their spears into pruning hooks; nations shall not lift up sword against nation, neither shall they learn war anymore. (Isaiah 2:4) But the first part of that verse was omitted from the marble wall. It tells how that will come to pass. It states, "And God shall judge among the nations and shall rebuke many people". Things of this world are in God's hands. He is God Most Holy. He is love and He is judge and His Millennial Reign is coming soon.

Eschatological Events in order:
- Rapture of the Church
- Great Tribulation
- Antichrist
- Coming of Christ to Earth
- Israel Saved
- Satan bound in the Bottomless Pit
- Millennial Reign of Christ
- Satan Loosed for a Season
- Great White Throne Judgment (for the lost)
- New Heaven and New Earth

Study Guide

CHAPTER SEVEN • THE COMING WORLD LEADER

Introduction

As we begin the second part of the Book of Daniel, we turn from history to prophecy. Our goals for this section are to have a synopsis of each chapter in our minds and to understand end time events.

1. List several ways in which God reveals his mind to men:

_____

_____

_____

_____

_____

_____

_____

_____

_____

2. Fill in the chart based on the first vision in Daniel 2 & Daniel 7.

World Empires (Daniel 2)	Symbolized (Daniel 2)	Symbolized Animal (Daniel 7) and appearance	Date
_____	_____	_____	_____
_____	_____	_____	_____
_____	_____	_____	_____
_____	_____	_____	_____

3. We know that the beast or little horn is the world dictator or Antichrist. How do the following scriptures describe this Antichrist?

Daniel 7:8 _____

Daniel 8:23 _____

Daniel 9:26 _____

Revelation 6:2 _____

Revelation 13:1 _____

2 Thessalonians 2:3 _____

2 Thessalonians 2:8 _____

1 John 2:18 _____

4. List in chronological order the pre-millennial events of the end time. _____

_____

_____

_____

_____

5. Define the term Antichrist. _____

_____

_____

Notice the characteristics that make the world dictator so appealing to the masses.

1. He is arrogant (verses 8, 20).
2. He is attractive and handsome (verse 20).
3. He is authoritative (verses 21, 25).
4. He has eyes that see all (he has legal control).
5. He has an amazing speaking ability (he has political control).
6. He has social graces and is very intelligent
   (he has social control).
7. Yet, he hates the Jews and all who support the Jews.
8. He is called a terrible beast (Daniel 7:7-8).

6. Who is the unholy trinity in Daniel and Revelation? _____

_____

_____

7. Who is the Ancient of Days and what does he do in Daniel 7?

_____

_____

_____

8. Explain the scene when Isaiah saw the Ancient of Days (Isaiah 6).

_____

_____

_____

9. Review the scene when Ezekiel saw the Ancient of Days (Ezekiel 1).

_____

_____

_____

10. What gift does the Ancient of Days give Jesus? _____

11. Compare Daniel 7:13 with Mark 14. This gift could be called the fifth kingdom. Why? _____

_____

The interpretation of the vision is this:
• 10 Horns symbolize 10 rulers who come out of a region once controlled by Rome (Revelation 13:1, 17:12).
• Another shall rise, "the little horn" or Antichrist and conquer three of the ten horns (kings) as head of a federation of nations.
• He will speak against the true God (2 Thessalonians 2:4) and per secute the saints, verse 25).
• He will come to a sudden and disastrous, horrible fate from the Ancient of Days.
• Christ's millennial reign on earth will begin.

12. According to Revelation 12:9 who is the dragon who gave the beast his power? _____

13. The saints are referred to as the children of the _____.

14. In Daniel 7:25 the terms time, times and one-half time refer to what length of time? _____

_____

15. Define these terms:

A millennial _____

_____

Pre-millennial _____

_____

Postmillennial _____

_____

The study of prophecy is not for vain knowledge but for careful and prayerful study of prophetic scripture to have a transforming effect on the life of the believer.

Sing the old Hymns:

"O Worship the King"
O worship the King, all glorious above,
O gratefully sing His power and His love;
Our Shield and Defender, the Ancient of Days
Pavilioned in splendor, and girded with praise.
1833 Words: Robert Grant, Music: Johann Hayden (Public Domain)

"Come Thou Almighty King"
Come Thou Almighty King
Help us Thy name to sing,
Help us to praise!
Father all-glorious
Over all victorious
Come and reign over us
Ancient of Days
1885 Felice de Giardini, Charles Wesley (Public Domain)

Visions of Daniel

First Vision	Second Vision	Third Vision	Fourth Vision
King: Belshazzar 1st year Date: 555 B.C. Daniel 7	King: Belshazzar 3rd Year Date: 552 B.C. Daniel 8	King: Darius 1st Year Date: 538 B.C. Daniel 9	King: Cyrus 3rd Year Date: 536 B.C. Daniel 10-12
Describe Vision: Panoramic Gentile world history Destinies of nations of world 4 great empires History at climax God's Kingdom established on earth His Son reigns Vision in Chapter 2 to pagan king and man would view it. Vision Chapter 7 as given to man of God as God sees things.	**Describe Vision:**	**Describe Vision:**	**Describe Vision:**

Millennium Views
Chapter 7 Appendix

The Fact of the Millennium
- This is a Latin word which means 1,000 years • Revelation 20:4.
- In Revelation 20, millennium is mentioned 6 times.

Postmillennialism
- Made popular by Unitarian Minister Daniel Whitby, 1638-1726.
- No longer considered in 20th Century because of WWI and Hitler's gas ovens in WWII.
- This belief that the world would get better and better and embrace Christianity and become a society of saints. This view was finally laid to rest because the Bible teaches the world will become worse and worse prior to Christ coming — 1 Timothy 4:1 and 2 Timothy 3:1-5.

A millennialism
- No thousand year reign at all.
- New Testament Church inherits promises and prophecies of Old Testament.

Premillennialism
- Christ will return just prior to the millennium
- Christ will personally rule during the glorious thousand year reign
- This is the oldest view and widely accepted as the scripturally correct one

Historic Premillennialists believe the church will go through the tribulation period. After the tribulation Christ will return to earth to establish a millennial kingdom. Believers who have died will be raised from the dead and their bodies reunited with their spirits. Believers will reign with Christ for one thousand years. (Wayne Gruden's Systematic Theology)

Dispensational Premillennialism

The rapture of the church takes place before the Tribulation period (7 years) or at the middle of the Tribulation(3 1/2 years). At the rapture the church is taken to heaven, leaving the judgments and promises of God to fall on unrepentant humanity and national Israel.

Both Premillennial views agree about the events at the end of the thousand years. Satan will be loosed from the bottomless pit and will join forces with unbelievers in their rebellion. Satan will gather forces for a battle against Christ and they will be completely defeated.

Christ will raise from the dead all unbelievers throughout history and they will stand before Him for the final judgment. Saints will enter the eternal state.

Chapter Eight

Power Shift Among Nations

The Bible warns us regarding the Antichrist that,
"By peace he will destroy many." Daniel 8:25.
Satan must direct this worship to Himself. The Bible
has warned us that Satan will attempt to exalt
his man, the Antichrist, over Christ. Islam does
exalt Mohammed above Christ and downgrades
Christ; likewise, the Mahdi is believed to have
the same attributes, and will also occupy the
Temple Mount. All this is written in the Islamic annals.

Page 142
God's War on Terror
Walid Shoebat with Joel Richardson

An important change takes place with this chapter. Daniel writes in Hebrew and for the last half of the book, he is writing about God's plan for Israel. This new vision takes place two years after the one Daniel had in chapter 7. Both visions were in the time of Belshazzar who was the last king of Babylon. During this vision, Daniel himself was living in Shushan or Susa, a very insignificant place at the time. It would soon be the capital of the Mede and Persian Empire. This city was also the home to Esther and Nehemiah.

The vision in this chapter is about the second and third world empires - the Medo-Persian and the Greek Empires. The events of this vision actually were fulfilled within two hundred years of Daniel's life. The Dead Sea Scrolls discovered in 1947 confirm that the book of Daniel was written during Daniel's lifetime.

The Vision of the Ram and the Goat

(1) In the third year of the reign of King Belshazzar a vision appeared to me — to me, Daniel — after the one that appeared to me the first time.
(2) I saw in the vision, and it so happened while I was looking, that I was in Shushan, the citadel, which is in the province of

Elam; and I saw in the vision that I was by the River Ulai.

(3) Then I lifted my eyes and saw, and there, standing beside the river, was a ram which had two horns, and the two horns were high; but one was higher than the other, and the higher one came up last.

(4) I saw the ram pushing westward, northward, and southward, so that no animal could withstand him; nor was there any that could deliver from his hand, but he did according to his will and became great.

(5) And as I was considering, suddenly a male goat came from the west, across the surface of the whole earth, without touching the ground; and the goat had a notable horn between his eyes.

(6) Then he came to the ram that had two horns, which I had seen standing beside the river, and ran at him with furious power.

(7) And I saw him confronting the ram; he was moved with rage against him, attacked the ram, and broke his two horns. There was no power in the ram to withstand him, but he cast him down to the ground and trampled him; and there was no one that could deliver the ram from his hand.

(8) Therefore the male goat grew very great; but when he became strong, the large horn was broken, and in place of it four notable ones came up toward the four winds of heaven.

- Daniel 8: 1-8

In the vision Daniel saw a ram with the usual two horns. The strange thing was that while Daniel watched, one horn grew and became higher than the other. Then this ram moved in three directions west, north and south. It could not be stopped and it became irresistible. This, of course, represents the Medo-Persian

Empire. The Persians grew stronger than the Medes and conquered to the west, north, and south. Cyrus and his son Cambyses II were thought to be invincible.

Another animal, a he-goat, appeared in the vision and challenged the ram. This strong buck of a goat had a conspicuous horn between his eyes. The goat was so swift that his feet did not touch the ground.

The fight was a great clash in which the ram was defeated. The outcome was that the goat became very strong, but at the height of its strength and power–the horn is broken off, and in its place four prominent horns appear and extend in four directions.

The goat represents Greece and the "great horn" symbolizes the first king, Alexander the Great. The four horns which replace it are the four kingdoms that replace Alexander's dominion.

Alexander defeated the Persians near Nineveh and verse 7 says that he "cast him (the ram) to the ground and stomped on him." When this empire was under his feet, he swept eastward to India but finally returned to Babylon where he died in 323 B.C., a victim of a fever (maybe malaria) and riotous living. He was 33 years old when he died.

Alexander's armies fought 20 years before the conquests were divided among 4 generals. The division was as follows:

Cassander	Ruled Macedonia, Greece, married to Alexander's sister
Lysimacthus	Ruled Turkey, parts Asia Minor
Seleucus	Ruled Syria, Israel, Mesopotamia
Ptolemy	Ruled Egypt, North Africa

The key to this vision is that a ruler out of the line of Seleucus will affect the fate of the Jews.

The Vision of the Little Horn

(9) And out of one of them came a little horn which grew exceedingly great toward the south, toward the east, and toward the Glorious Land.
(10) And it grew up to the host of heaven; and it cast down some of the host and some of the stars to the ground, and trampled them.
(11) He even exalted himself as high as the Prince of the host; and by him the daily sacrifices were taken away, and the place of His sanctuary was cast down.
(12) Because of transgression, an army was given over to the horn to oppose the daily sacrifices; and he cast truth down to the ground. He did all this and prospered.
(13) Then I heard a holy one speaking; and another holy one said to that certain one who was speaking, "How long will the vision be, concerning the daily sacrifices and the trans-gression of desolation, the giving of both the sanctuary and the host to be trampled underfoot?"
(14) And he said to me, "For two thousand three hundred days; [a] then the sanctuary shall be cleansed."
- Daniel 8: 9-14

As Daniel's vision continues, he sees a "little horn" or ruler coming out of the four generals under Alexander. This ruler is Antiochus IV Epiphanes, 8th in the line of successors from Seleucus and he reigned in Syria from 175-164 B.C. Notice with me that the prophecy skips from 301 when the generals divide the empire to 175 when Antiochus Epiphanes becomes the king.

He is not the little horn of chapter 7. They are not the same because the little horn of chapter 7 rises out of the Roman Empire in the end times and the little horn of chapter 8 springs from the Grecian Empire in the ancient times. They are both called horns which are symbolic of ruling or power.

They are alike in that they hated the Jewish people and profaned their temple and the one true Holy God. This happened in the time between the Old and New Testaments. However, this Antiochus Epiphanes is a foreshadowing of the Antichrist of chapter 7 who is the enemy of the Jews in the Tribulation. He is ruler over the Promised Land, the precious land or the glorious land, that God loved above all others and set aside for the Jews.

About the Man Antiochus Epiphanes

- He murdered his brother to obtain the throne. He called himself "god manifest" on his coins.
- He profaned the temple in Jerusalem (Dan. 11:31) and he attempted to destroy the city.
- These attempts are recorded in world history and in 1 and 2 Maccabees of the Apocrypha.
- He plundered the temple's treasury and butchered multiplied thousands of inhabitants of Jerusalem.
- In 167 B.C he sacked the city, destroyed the walls and issued edicts that prevented Jews from following their customs such as circumcisions, worship, honoring the Sabbath, following dietary regulations or offering sacrifices.
- He offered a pig on the holy altar of the temple and made a new altar to Zeus. He also rode on the back of a pig in the Temple.

Verses 10 and 11 describe his evil activities. He stole everything of value out of the temple. He caused all daily sacrifices to stop. Thus the true religion was "cast to the ground" and paganism was substituted for Judaism.

Antiochus withdrew to Persia where he became insane and died. He was a forerunner to the Antichrist of Revelation. He was vicious, wicked and full of Satan's iniquity.

He called himself Epiphanes–the glorious one or illustrious one–but the Jews, using a play on words, changed the "n" to an "m" and called him Epimanes, which meant the mad man. The Maccabees rose up to revolt against him to restore their temple worship and their nation. They endured this extermination attempt for 6.5 years.

About Hanukkah

After 6.5 years, in the month of December in 165 B.C., the temple was restored and cleansed by the Maccabees. One day's supply of oil miraculously kept the golden lamp stand burning for 8 days. That cleansing has since been celebrated as the Feast of Dedication (John 10:22) or Hanukkah. God used the Maccabees to bring about the end of the astounding devastation of Antiochus IV (Dan. 8:24).

What is now history to us was prophecy to Daniel. He would not live to see this prophecy fulfilled but he received the revelation with such certain facts that he "was exhausted and lay ill for several days" following the revelation. It is so accurate that even today if we could fully grasp what we hear on the news regarding the global situation which is preparing this world for that horrible "master of intrigue," that wicked antichrist to come, we like Daniel, would be ill, sick and sick at heart.

The Vision Interpreted by Gabriel

Then it happened, when I, Daniel, had seen the vision and
was seeking the meaning, that suddenly there stood before
me one having the appearance of a man. And I heard a man's
voice between the banks of the Ulai, who called, and said,
"Gabriel, make this man understand the vision." So he came
near where I stood, and when he came I was afraid and fell
on my face; but he said to me, "Understand, son of man, that
the vision refers to the time of the end."
Now, as he was speaking with me, I was in a deep sleep with
my face to the ground; but he touched me, and stood me
upright. And he said, "Look, I am making known to you what
shall happen in the latter time of the indignation; for at the
appointed time the end shall be.
- Daniel 8: 15-19

One stood before Daniel with the appearance of a man. From
a distance a voice spoke to Gabriel commanding him to make this
man understand the vision. The sound of the voice came from the
canal of the Ulai River and between its banks the voice hovered in
the air. Many scholars say this was the voice of God. Others
believe it was the voice of the pre-incarnate Christ.

This is the first time in the Bible an angel is given a name.
Gabriel means "strong one". Daniel falls on his face. Daniel was in
a deep sleep or coma. He had fallen out in the Spirit. It was too
holy for him to grasp. The angel touched Daniel in v. 18 and raised
him to his feet. Gabriel said twice it pertains to the time of the
end. The term indignation is God's judgment on his people. Even
though this time 171-165 B.C. was a horrible time of persecution,
it did not mark the time of the end because the Jews even today

continue to be persecuted and the end is not yet come.

We see in Antiochus Epiphanes a dreadful picture of the Antichrist to come in the end time. While the chapter describes the evil character and deeds of Antiochus (Antichrist of the Old Testament) it also is clear that he foreshadows the Antichrist of the New Testament. This is called Double Fulfillment, a far reaching truth and a near reaching truth. It lays one thing beside another. It presents two things at once. The ultimate Antichrist is much worse than the one in Daniel.

> *So when you see standing in the holy place 'the abomination that causes desolation, spoken of through the prophet Daniel — let the reader understand—*
> - Matthew 24:15

Christ makes reference to Daniel and says when this abomination of desolation happens, simply run for your life and don't stop to gather anything to take with you.

The abomination of desolation is to come. It will be driven by Satan, the Dragon, who is a master of intrigue and master of riddles. As we learned in the last chapter, when the Antichrist takes a stand against the Lord Jesus Christ, he is destroyed by the word out of the mouth of Christ in Revelation 19:20 I truly believe the Antichrist will not come until the restrainer is taken away and that restrainer is the body of Christ on earth, the church.

The two, Satan and the Antichrist, will be alike in the following ways:

1) Appear in the latter time of their kingdom
2) Appear when the transgressions are full –deep trials coming called Jacob's troubles

3) Appear as king of fierce countenance and understanding dark sentences-foreboding, brilliant mind, solving hard problems
4) Great power due to Satanic control
5) Try to destroy the mighty and holy people
6) Practice deceit to accomplish purposes
7) Exalts Himself (2 Thess. 2:4)
8) Promise peace and security but will bring destruction
9) Oppose the Prince of princes v. 25 – God and Christ the Messiah
10) Destroyed but not by human power (v.25) when Christ returns to earth.

The Effect of the Vision on Daniel

And I, Daniel, fainted and was sick for days; afterward I arose and went about the king's business. I was astonished by the vision, but no one understood it.
- Daniel 8:27

Here is proof positive that sickness Is not always a result of sin. Sickness may come from Satan or as judgment for sin in Exodus 15:26. It may come because we take the Lord's Supper without being worthy as in 1 Corinthians 11:30 or as in Daniel's situation, it may be produced as a superabundance of divine revelation and sympathy with the sorrowful stricken saints of God. Daniel had such personal sympathy with what would happen to his own people because of their sin that he fainted and was sick several days. He wept with sorrow.

God is a just and holy, loving and merciful God who has provided a way of salvation whereby you may be saved by looking to the Lord Jesus Christ and trusting Him before the awful and terrible conflict that is coming. Receive Him now! "Believe on the Lord Jesus Christ, and thou shalt be saved."

Study Guide

CHAPTER EIGHT • POWER SHIFT AMONG NATIONS

Introduction

We explored a new vision in this chapter. There is an important shift to note at this point in the book. Daniel interpreted the King's dreams earlier in the book but now God is giving Daniel the visions and the interpretations.

Read verses 1-8 and then the interpretation of this vision in verses 9-27.

1. The Two-Horned Ram is _____

2. The two horns are the two king's _____

and _____

3. The Shaggy Goat is the kingdom of _____

4. This kingdom's greatest king, the large horn, was _____

5. How and when did this great king die? _____

6. Upon his death, four horns came out of this kingdom.
Name them.

_____ King of Macedonia and Greece

_____ King of Thrace and parts of Asia Minor

_____ King of Egypt and parts of Asia Minor

_____ King of Syria, Israel, Mesopotamia

For our study, the most important of these kings is Seleucus, the king over Israel. He killed his brother to become king. He is Seleucus IV and was also known as Antiochus Epiphanes.

7. The word Epiphanes means _____.

8. The Jewish people called him Epimanes (a play on words) meaning _____.

9. In verse 9, the glorious land is what land? _____

Remember from Chapter 7 that the "Little Horn" is the Antichrist and he comes out of the Roman Empire. So this large horn is not the final Beast or dragon (Satan). Chapter 7 is a prophecy of the Antichrist and Chapter 8 is Antiochus IV. Which is a more immediate prophecy? In Daniel's day this was prophecy. For us today it is history.

Since Antiochus foreshadows the Antichrist (sometimes referred to as the beast). The term's dual reference and double ful-fillment are used by commentaries. One is near-reaching and the other is far-reaching.

10. Read and paraphrase Matthew 24:15. When this happens, what does Jesus say to do? _____•_____

_____

_____

What things does Antiochus Epiphanes do?

11. Verse 23 states he is a master of what? _____

12. Verses 22-25 state he destroys the holy people. How? _____

_____

_____

13. He desolates the people and the temple. How? _____

_____

_____

14. He stands against the Prince of Princes. How? _____

_____

_____

Prophecy: Double Fulfillment

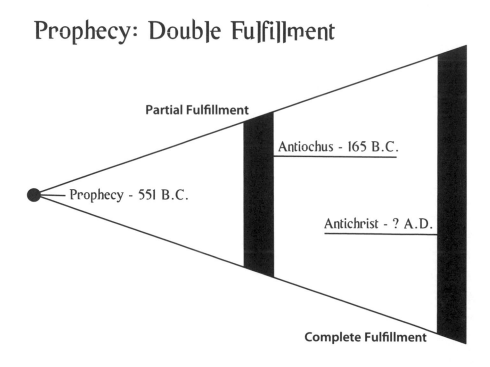

Partial Fulfillment

Antiochus - 165 B.C.

Prophecy - 551 B.C.

Antichrist - ? A.D.

Complete Fulfillment

Chapter Nine
The Seventy Week Countdown

D aniel lived in captivity for all of his adult life. He served under three kings and two kingdoms and found favor in every situation. We have watched as he was severely tested but always faithful to Jehovah God. The secret to Daniel's loyalty and devotion was his prayer life. He prayed for illumination and interpretation in Daniel 2. He prayed when he defied the King's decree in Daniel 6. Now we find him praying a prayer of confession and humiliation for his people in chapter 9.

INTRODUCTION

The prophecy of Daniel's seventy weeks of years is the most remarkable of all Biblical prophecies besides the birth of Christ. Dr. Alva McClain cites the importance of this prophecy:

> 1. This prophecy has huge evidential value as a witness to the truth of the scripture. This prophecy predicts the EXACT day in which our Messiah rode into the city of Jerusalem as God's Prince.
> 2. This prophecy is the strong rock on which theories of prophecy are shattered. There are those who deny predictions in prophecy but Daniel's clear predictions of future historical events will destroy all unbelief.

3. This prophecy is the undisputable chronological key to all New Testament prophecy. The great prophetic announcements in Matthew 24 and Mark 13 are those prophecies tied to Daniel's remarkable prophecy of the 70th week of years. In addition to that, the Book of Revelation speaks of a final 7 years under such description as 1260 days, two periods of 42 months, and two periods of 3.5 years.

Circumstances When the Prophecy was Delivered

Daniel grew old as a captive in Babylon. While studying Jeremiah 25:11, Daniel discovered that the captivity set for 70 years was coming to an end.

And this whole land shall be a desolation and an astonishment, and these nations shall serve the King of Babylon seventy years.
- Jeremiah 25:11

Having made this discovery (Daniel 9:2), Daniel prayed to God concerning his city (Jerusalem) and his people (Israel). He may have realized that all God's promises to his nation were not going to be fulfilled during his own lifetime. He must have understood that he was not going to be able to return to Jerusalem. He was in anguish over Israel and its future. Being homesick and longing for Israel made his prayer even more painful. He was mourning for his country. Look back at Daniel 9:3-19.

So Daniel put on sackcloth and ashes, and began to pray intensely for God's will. He addressed God as a great and awesome God, a faithful and righteous God, a just, merciful and forgiving God, a mighty God and a God who had heard and continues to answer prayers. He prays "O Lord". He begs God to glorify Himself by blessing His people and blessing His Holy City, Jerusalem, again.

The Angelic Visitation • Daniel 9:20-27

God then miraculously and gloriously sent Gabriel to give him a most amazing prophecy which contained the date of the first coming of Christ. It is interesting that 445 years later this same angel Gabriel will appear before the Virgin Mary to announce that she will have a son and call his name Jesus.

Notice in verses 21 and 22 Gabriel, who came to him in chapter 8, comes to him in late afternoon around the time of the evening sacrifice to inform him and give him skill to understand this supernatural message! If we cannot embrace the supernatural, then our lives will simply be superficial. Daniel was qualified to hear from Gabriel because he BELIEVED. Lord help our unbelief so we may embrace you fully as Daniel did.

The Prophetic Revelation • Daniel 9:24-27

(24) Seventy weeks are determined For your people and for your holy city, to finish the transgression, to make an end of sins, to make reconciliation for iniquity, to bring in everlasting righteousness, to seal up vision and prophecy, and to anoint the Most Holy.
(25) Know therefore and understand, that from the going forth of the command to restore and build Jerusalem until

Messiah the Prince, there shall be seven weeks and sixty-two weeks; the street shall be built again, and the wall, even in troublesome times.

(26) And after the sixty-two weeks Messiah shall be cut off, but not for Himself; and the people of the prince who is to come shall destroy the city and the sanctuary. The end of it shall be with a flood, and till the end of the war desolations are determined.

(27) Then he shall confirm a covenant with many for one week; but in the middle of the week He shall bring an end to sacrifice and offering. And on the wing of abominations shall be one who makes desolate, even until the consummation, which is determined, is poured out on the desolate.
- Daniel 9:24-27 (NKJV)

To the casual reader the 70 weeks would seem to be 70 periods of 7 days. But that is not the case! When we look at the Hebrew we discover that the word "week" is not there. The Hebrew word shabua simply means seven. Daniel 9:24 should read "Seventy Sevens are determined upon thy people and thy city…" The Jewish people understood this concept.

• The Jews understood that they could till the ground, gather fruit and prune their vineyards for 6 years. But the Sabbath, or 7th year, was a year to let the land rest and that would be holy to the Lord. Leviticus 25:3-4

• The Jews understood that they continued for seven Sabbaths of years (7X7) = 49 years, but the 50th was called Jubilee and all debts were cancelled, estates were returned and slaves freed. It was a year of celebration and rejoicing.

Daniel knew that one of the reasons the Jews had been removed from the land was their violation of the sabbatical year. For 490 years they had disobeyed God and abused the land. God now claimed His 70th Sabbath. The land enjoyed its sabbath rests; all the time of its desolation it rested, until the seventy years were completed in fulfillment of the word of the LORD spoken by Jeremiah. 2 Chronicles 36:21

Jehovah God was beginning a new era of 490 years for the Jews and Jerusalem. Daniel's 70 weeks of years is 490 years. (70x7 = 490)

How long then are these years? Our calendar year has 365.25 days. (Leap Year every 4 years) But in the Old Testament and the Jewish calendar or lunar calendar. every month had exactly 30 days. In Revelation and Daniel all of these are the same: 3.5 years, 42 months and 1260 days. So in conclusion 490, years are years of 360 days each.

69 Weeks of Years Begins and Ends - WHEN?

Let me remind you that Daniel's people are the Jews and Daniel's city is Jerusalem. (v. 25) Notice in verse 26 there are two different ones called "prince" "After the sixty-two 'sevens,' the Anointed One will be put to death and will have nothing. The people of the ruler who will come will destroy the city and the sanctuary. The end will come like a flood: War will continue until the end, and desolations have been decreed."

There is Messiah in verse 25 and the coming Prince in verse 26. The 70 weeks of years are divided into 3 periods. The first two periods total 69 weeks of years, and the final period is 1 week of years, or 7 years.

Daniel 9:25 states "at the going forth of the commandment to restore and to build Jerusalem shall be 7 weeks and 62 weeks." Now do not get confused here. The commandment is NOT to rebuild the temple, but the commandment is to REBUILD THE CITY. There is only one decree in all of the Old Testament that can be called a commandment to rebuild a city.

(1) The words of Nehemiah the son of Hachaliah.
It came to pass in the month of Chislev, in the twentieth year, as I was in Shushan the citadel,
(2) that Hanani one of my brethren came with men from Judah; and I asked them concerning the Jews who had escaped, who had survived the captivity, and concerning Jerusalem.
(3) And they said to me, "The survivors who are left from the captivity in the province are there in great distress and reproach. The wall of Jerusalem is also broken down, and its gates are burned with fire."
(4) So it was, when I heard these words, that I sat down and wept, and mourned for many days; I was fasting and praying before the God of heaven.
- Nehemiah 1:1-4 (NKJV)

(1) And it came to pass in the month of Nisan, in the twentieth year of King Artaxerxes, when wine was before him, that I took the wine and gave it to the king. Now I had never been sad in his presence before.
(2) Therefore the king said to me, "Why is your face sad, since you are not sick? This is nothing but sorrow of heart." So I became dreadfully afraid,
(3) and said to the king, "May the king live forever! Why

should my face not be sad, when the city, the place of my
fathers' tombs, lays waste, and its gates are burned with fire?"
(4) Then the king said to me, "What do you request?"
So I prayed to the God of heaven.
(5) And I said to the king, "If it pleases the king, and if your ser-
vant has found favor in your sight, I ask that you send me to
Judah, to the city of my fathers' tombs, that I may rebuild it."
(6) Then the king said to me (the queen also sitting beside
him), "How long will your journey be? And when will you
return?" So it pleased the king to send me; and I set him a
time.
(7) Furthermore I said to the king, "If it pleases the king, let let-
ters be given to me for the governors of the region beyond the
River, that they must permit me to pass through till I come to
Judah,
(8) and a letter to Asaph the keeper of the king's forest, that
he must give me timber to make beams for the gates of the
citadel which pertains to the temple, for the city wall, and for
the house that I will occupy." And the king granted them to
me according to the good hand of my God upon me.
- Nehemiah 2:1-8 (NKJV)

Nehemiah receives the command from King Artaxerxes and gives us the exact date in Nehemiah 2:1, "in the month of Nisan in the 20 years of Artaxerxes the king." From secular history we know that Artaxerxes had his coronation in 465 B.C. Thus marking the date that Nehemiah had the signed papers to go to Jerusalem to rebuild it on March 14, 445 B.C.

With this information we can figure out the end of the 69 weeks of years. We take 69 x 7 x 360 and we come up with 173,880 days. We begin with the first day of Nisan, so on the Jewish calendar, the 60 weeks of years ends on April 6, 32 A.D.

Daniel's prophecy declares that this would be the day of Messiah being presented as Prince of Israel.   April 6, 32 A.D. is Nisan 10, the day we call Palm Sunday, the day our Lord rode into Jerusalem on the donkey fulfilling the prophecy in Zechariah 9:9, "Rejoice greatly, Daughter Zion!

Shout, Daughter Jerusalem! See, your king comes to you, righteous and victorious, lowly and riding on a donkey, on a colt, the foal of a donkey." New Testament accounts of the Triumphant Entry are found in Matthew 21:1-11, Mark 11:1-11 and John 12:12-19.

Our Lord Jesus weeps because the Jews missed the time of His visitation to them.

- 7 weeks of years - 7 x 7 = 49 weeks of years
- Sixty-two weeks of years - 62 x 7=434 weeks of years
- 49 plus 434 = 483
- One week of years (not yet happened) 1 x 7 = 7
  occur after the rapture
- 483 + 7 = 490 weeks of years.

When Jesus made that entry into Jerusalem on a donkey and wept, it was because the Jews would reject him and Jerusalem would be destroyed. This was the end of the 69 weeks or the 173,880 days. After this, the Messiah is cut off or crucified in A.D. 33 for our sins. John 1:11 says, "He came to His own, and His own did not receive Him. But as many as received Him, to them He gave the right to become children of God to those who believe in His name." (See also Daniel 9:26)

As stated, the first 69 weeks of years ended when Jesus presented himself to Israel. Now because Israel rejected him as Messiah, the 70th week of years has been delayed or put on hold.

It is as if the prophetic clock for Israel has stopped until the 70th begins. We are living in this gap of time now- the unlabeled weeks of years known as the church age. When the Jews rejected Christ, the church age clock started ticking. This is called the age of grace. An unspecified gap of time is not unusual in scripture. Isaiah tells us, "For unto us a child is born," which we know happened over two thousand years ago. The next phrase says, "and the government shall be upon his shoulders," and we know that in the future this will take place.

The Last Week of Years Will Begin & End - WHEN?

The final seven years are yet to come. The scripture uses terms like: Jacob's Trouble, Day of Wrath and Great Tribulation to describe this last segment of history. In Daniel 9:26 we find the destruction of Jerusalem by the people of a "coming prince." Of course Rome destroyed Jerusalem in 70 A.D as Jesus foretold. A coming prince during these last 7 years will be called the Antichrist.

These last seven years will contain all the prophesies of this wicked one who is like Satan. He will be a charming, handsome, diplomatic, smooth talker with a magnetic personality. People will follow and believe everything he says. When this happens, the church age is over and the church will be removed in the rapture.

In Matthew 24 our Lord Jesus affirmed that Daniel's prophecy of the 70th week was yet to be. Jesus said when the abomination of desolation occurs in the temple in Jerusalem, it will be the onset of the Great Tribulation which will be followed by the second coming of Christ.

When the Antichrist appears, God will restart Israel's prophetic clock. The beginning of the Great Tribulation is a seven year covenant between the Beast (Antichrist) and the Jewish people. It is a peace accord of sorts; the Antichrist will promise peace but will not deliver. We know that only Jesus brings real peace. He is the true Prince of Peace. Without Christ true peace cannot be found. (Read Matthew 24:15, Mark 13:14-23, Luke 17:23, 24, 37; 21:20-24).

After three and one half years of the seven year covenant with Israel, the Antichrist will break the covenant, stop their sacrificial system, and begin intense persecution of the Jews. He will commit that abomination which is to violate the holy temple in Jerusalem. Antichrist had been Israel's protector and now he has become Israel's persecutor.

He will place an image of himself on the high and holy altar of the temple in the Holy of Holies. Antichrist will proclaim he is god and insist that the world worship him (reads like Nebuchadnezzar of chapter 2). At the end of the 70th week of years, a time of blessing will come upon Israel. We call this the millennium. At the end of the 70 weeks in Revelation 19:11-24, Christ shall appear coming through the clouds on a white horse. He will wear a robe dipped in blood and with a word defeat the Antichrist, the false prophet and Satan himself.

God's word is remarkable and always true. There is one God and Jesus Christ is his name. When Daniel said the Messiah was cut off—that meant he died for each of us—crucified for our sins. The accuracy of scripture is astonishing. God gave exact dates to Daniel. All of this is true, verified in history and in the prophecies of the Holy Scripture.

Study  Guide

CHAPTER NINE • THE SEVENTY WEEKS COUNTDOWN

Introduction

Notice that the events of chapter nine took place after the fall of Babylon and in the first year of the reign of Darius. This was around the same time as the lion's den experience. In the beginning of this chapter we learned that Daniel was not only a prophet but also a student of prophecy. He studied the Holy Scriptures and found time to pray three times a day. How much more then should we study since we have the entire Bible and he only had a portion of it?

1. Daniel began to intercede for the nation Israel while reading the book of _____.

2. Which angel came to Daniel while he prayed? _____

3. Why did the angel come? _____

_____

4. By what title was Daniel greeted? _____

5. To whom did the angel Gabriel visit in the New Testament and why? _____

_____

_____

Define these words:

6. Apologetics _____

_____

7. Eschatology _____

_____

8. Prophecy _____

_____

9. In Daniel 9:24, it was decreed that God would cut out a period of time specifically for the people of _____ and the city of _____.

After reading verse 24, list the 6 critical fulfillments that will accomplish "God's purpose in history."

10. "to _____ transgression"

11. "to bring in everlasting _____"

12. "to put an _____ to sin"

13. "to _____ up vision and prophecy"

14. "to _____ for wickedness"

15. "to _____ the most holy"

During this, Israel will come to the end of rebellion against Christ. The angel gave insight and understanding to Daniel about end times.

Here, we read three different prophecies concerning "seven".

16. The first is 7 sevens (7 years x 7) is equal to _____ years.

17. 62 sevens (62 years x 7) is equal to _____ years.

18. One seven is equal to _____ years.

19. The Jewish calendar is a lunar calendar with a 360 day year which is different from our 365 days. Daniel learns from the Angel Gabriel that this segment of time was set to begin with the decree to restore and _____ Jerusalem (not the temple but the city).

Read Nehemiah 2:1 which sets the date in the month of Nisan in the 20th year of King Artaxerxes. The actual figured date was March 5. Nisan is March/April on our calendar. It took 49 years to completely, thoroughly restore Jerusalem "with streets and a trench".

The 62 years x 7 years, or 434 years, would last until "the Anointed One" or in Hebrew "Messiah" (Masiyah) would be proclaimed on Palm Sunday.

20. Read Luke 19:29-40 and explain. _____

_____

_____

_____

21. A 483 year period contains how many days? _____

22. Paraphrase what happened in Nehemiah 1 and 2 on March 5, 444 B.C. _____

_____

_____

_____

23. In Daniel 9:26 "after" signals a gap in time. After the 62 sevens, the Anointed One will be _____.

24. What does John 1:12 refer to? _____

_____

25. The third mention of seven is the final block that begins with a covenant between the little horn (beast) of chapter 7 and the people of _____.

Let me remind you that in the middle of the final seven years there is a critical point.

- time, times and half-time = 3.5 years
- forty-two months = 3.5 years
- 1,260 days = 3.5 years

The Antichrist and Israel will make a 7 year pact for peace but it will be disregarded after 3.5 years because peace is only found in Jesus Christ.

26. What does the Antichrist do in the middle of the pact with Israel? _____

_____

_____

27. Read and explain Matthew 24:15 _____

_____

_____

_____

28. Abomination means _____

_____

29. The Antichrist's conduct will continue until the Lord Jesus Christ will overthrow this beast-king. This closing verse refers to the Antichrist. Explain: _____

_____

_____

_____

_____

_____

Daniel's Prophecy of the 70 Weeks
by Dr. Alva J. McClain

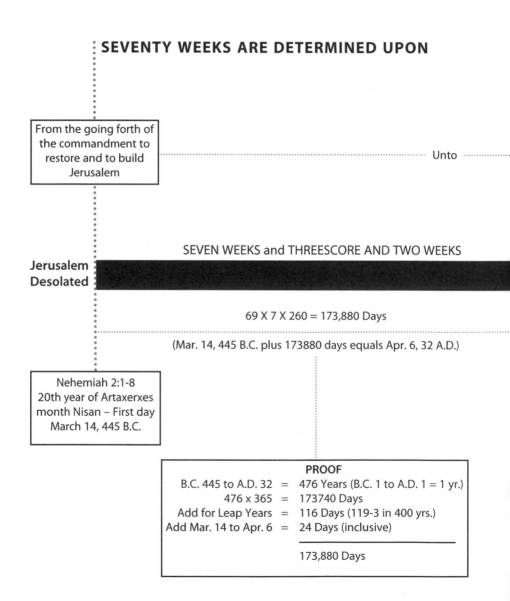

SEVENTY WEEKS ARE DETERMINED UPON

From the going forth of the commandment to restore and to build Jerusalem

Unto

Jerusalem Desolated

SEVEN WEEKS and THREESCORE AND TWO WEEKS

69 X 7 X 260 = 173,880 Days

(Mar. 14, 445 B.C. plus 173880 days equals Apr. 6, 32 A.D.)

Nehemiah 2:1-8
20th year of Artaxerxes
month Nisan – First day
March 14, 445 B.C.

PROOF

B.C. 445 to A.D. 32	=	476 Years (B.C. 1 to A.D. 1 = 1 yr.)
476 x 365	=	173740 Days
Add for Leap Years	=	116 Days (119-3 in 400 yrs.)
Add Mar. 14 to Apr. 6	=	24 Days (inclusive)

173,880 Days

THY PEOPLE AND UPON THY HOLY CITY

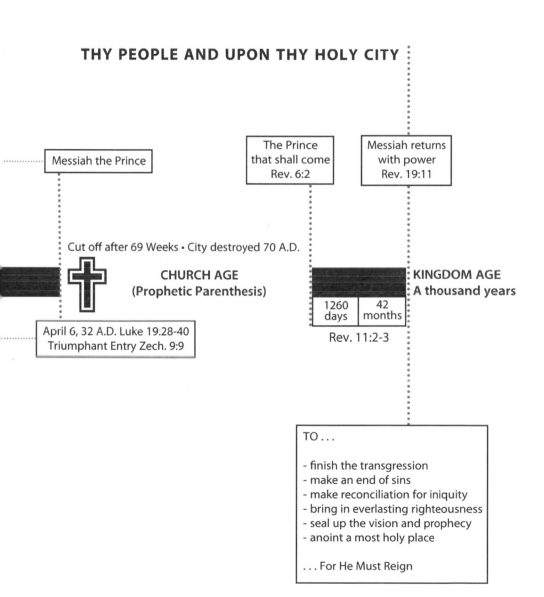

Messiah the Prince

The Prince
that shall come
Rev. 6:2

Messiah returns
with power
Rev. 19:11

Cut off after 69 Weeks • City destroyed 70 A.D.

CHURCH AGE
(Prophetic Parenthesis)

KINGDOM AGE
A thousand years

1260
days

42
months

Rev. 11:2-3

April 6, 32 A.D. Luke 19:28-40
Triumphant Entry Zech. 9:9

TO . . .

- finish the transgression
- make an end of sins
- make reconciliation for iniquity
- bring in everlasting righteousness
- seal up the vision and prophecy
- anoint a most holy place

. . . For He Must Reign

Chapter Ten

God's Glorious Touch

The purposes of the United Nations are:
to maintain international peace and security,
to take effective collective measures for the
prevention and removal of threats to the peace.

U.N. Charter 1945

These things I have spoken to you,
that in Me you may have peace.
In the world you have tribulation,
but take courage; I have over come the world.

Jesus Christ
King of Kings and Lord of Lords

The plans of God are wonderful, mysterious and meticulous. I pray that your faith has grown as you have persevered through this holy and prophetic book with enthusiasm and diligence.

Surely you have not been intimidated by this dedicated and spiritual man, Daniel. Because of Daniel's holy life and devotion to prayer, God chose to reveal to him the strange supernatural future events of this world. That should encourage all of us to pursue diligently our walk with God, prayer and a holy life.

As the last three chapters of Daniel unfold, we see the introduction to the vision in chapter 10, the vision itself in chapter 11 and the final words of the vision in chapter 12. This last section is one unit. Even though Daniel was around 85 years of age at this point, he had not outlived his usefulness to God. There is one last massive vision for the children of Israel. It will be seen and interpreted by Daniel.

The Burden • Daniel 10:1-4

In the first year of Cyrus's reign he signed a decree allowing all Jews freedom to return to their homeland in Israel. However, two years later only a small portion, approximately 50,000 Jews, had chosen to go home. Daniel was grieved that more of his people had not taken the opportunity to return to Israel.

However, conditions were horrible for those who returned there. (Ezra 1:1-4) The adversaries who occupied the land tried to discourage and trouble the Jews in the work of building their temple. These enemies even hired people to frustrate and annoy the people in their resolve to build the Temple. The desolate cities and poor living conditions further discouraged the people.

(1) In the third year of Cyrus king of Persia, a message was revealed to Daniel, whose name was called Belteshazzar. The message was true, but the appointed time was long; and he understood the message, and had understanding of the vision.
(2) In those days I, Daniel, was mourning three full weeks.
(3) I ate no pleasant food, no meat or wine came into my mouth, nor did I anoint myself at all, till three whole weeks were fulfilled.
(4) Now on the twenty-fourth day of the first month, as I was by the side of the great river, that is, the Tigris,
- Daniel 10:1-4

This vision occurred in 535 B.C. during the third year of the rule of Cyrus of the Mede and Persian Empire. It is believed that this vision came very near to the end of Daniel's life.

The supernatural encounter took place on April 24, as Daniel was standing by the Tigris River where he experienced a strange vision. He was deeply troubled and was beginning to understand that the fulfillment of God's promises to his nation was not going to occur during his lifetime. He himself was not going to be able to return to Jerusalem and he was in anguish over Israel and its future. This season was right after the Passover and at the end of Unleavened Bread. Trying to honor the holy days was sorrowful for an exile. He longed for home and the temple, which made his prayer more painful. Daniel continued to fast and pray for three more weeks. He was troubled that Israel had received permission to go home, but fewer than 50,000 actually returned in the two years. He was also troubled by the delay in God answering his prayer. Why aren't people willing to obey God quickly?

Doubtless, Daniel was troubled over many things. His dreams for Israel would not happen, at least not in his lifetime. He would not be a participant in the rebuilding of the temple. Why did God not answer his prayer for 21 days? No answer came until he was greatly weakened by hunger. But God came on the scene with a glorious vision of the pre-incarnate Christ.

He did not bathe for three weeks. He denied himself so he could pray and **fast**. He ate no meat and drank no wine. He was mourning over his country. I repent that I have never fasted and prayed for our own America for three weeks. Do I love America as much as Daniel loved Israel?

Have you ever been through a time when you thought God was absent and not listening to your prayer? Inside your troubled heart, did you say, "If God can hear, He must not care."? I am sure Daniel wondered why God was not answering his prayer. He was so desperate and hungry for a response from God.

The Theophany

Daniel's heart was about to be overwhelmed!

(5) I lifted my eyes and looked, and behold, a certain man clothed in linen, whose waist was girded with gold of Uphaz!
(6) His body was like beryl, his face like the appearance of

lightning, his eyes like torches of fire, his arms and feet like burnished bronze in color, and the sound of his words like the voice of a multitude.

(7) And I, Daniel, alone saw the vision, for the men who were with me did not see the vision; but a great terror fell upon them, so that they fled to hide themselves.

(8) Therefore I was left alone when I saw this great vision, and no strength remained in me; for my vigor was turned to frailty in me, and I retained no strength.

(9) Yet I heard the sound of his words; and while I heard the sound of his words I was in a deep sleep on my face, with my face to the ground.

- Daniel 10:5-9

Although the others with him at the banks of the Tigris did not see the vision with their eyes, they ran away in fear. The vision was meant for Daniel alone. If the vision is not meant for you or me, then we won't see it. This is similar to Saul's conversion experience in Acts 9 when he saw a blinding light, fell to the ground and heard the voice of Jesus. The men traveling with Saul heard a voice but did not see the vision. The vision was intended for Saul alone.

While we were in the Fresh Oil New Wine Conference at Abba's House, my brother Burt asked me during worship if I could see the outline of the face of Jesus. I was looking at the power point and singing so I said no. I did not know where he was looking. The next night, one of the speaker's wives was sitting beside me and asked before service if I had seen the outline of the face of Jesus the night before. I said no, but my brother said yes, he saw it in the baptistery. They had seen a vision and I had not. We don't see a vision just because someone else sees one. There are no second hand visions.

In this vision the Pre-incarnate Christ, (the Christophany), appeared to Daniel. He was wearing fine linen which was characteristic of a priest. His face was like lightning and his belt was made of gold. His great brilliance caused Daniel to fall down. When God comes near, we fall down before His splendid beauty. The sound of His words were heard by Daniel even though he was on his face in a coma–like state. When he had this vision of the Lord Jesus Christ, Daniel was alone.

No longer did Daniel see a vision of a statue, lion, bear, leopard, ram or goat. No longer did this prophet see ravenous beasts or weeks of time unfolding. The vision of the God-man, the Pre-incarnate Christ, was holy and overpowering! This experience had a tremendous effect on him which drained his strength and resulted in unconsciousness.

We call this type of manifestation in response to the power of God "falling out" or being "slain in the Spirit". His deep sleep was the result of the presence of God. The Apostle John had a similar experience as he saw the Christ in a vision on the Isle of Patmos in Revelation 1:12-18.

(17) When I saw him, I fell at his feet as though dead. Then he placed his right hand on me and said: "Do not be afraid. I am the First and the Last."
- Revelation 1: 17

Notice that the descriptions of John and Daniel's encounters are closely related. This is not a coincidence. No human can encounter the greatness of the manifest presence of God without having some type of physical response.

*(9) and while I heard the sound of his words I was in a deep
sleep on my face, with my face to the ground.
(10) Suddenly, a hand touched me, which made me tremble
on my knees and on the palms of my hands.*
- Daniel 10:9-10

When Daniel awoke, the pre-incarnate Christ was gone but an
angel had touched him and caused him to tremble on his knees
and hands. Have you felt that tremble in times of ministry? When
God reveals His presence, your mind and body cannot contain
the glory. I have seen others shake uncontrollably under the
power of God. I have experienced that myself and have known it
was all about God's presence. The angel touched him. A heavenly
touch reveals that we are greatly loved, that we have understanding, that we do not have to fear, that we have ability to pray, and
that we can understand scripture.

The Angels

Angels are created spiritual beings with high intelligence, moral
judgments and without bodies. They take on a bodily form when
sent to man.

Demons

Demons are evil, fallen angels that oppose God and are the
enemy of God. Satan, who was the anointed cherub, through his
pride wanted all that God had; his desire was to be God. He revolt-
ed against the God of heaven and took 1/3 of the heavenly hosts

with him. Demons have moral judgments and exercise those judgments in opposition to God.

For a complete study of angels and demons I recommend Ron Phillips' books on these subjects: *Angels: Our Invisible Allies and Everyone's Guide to Demons and Spiritual Warfare*. www.ron-phillips.org.

The angel spoke to Daniel, calling him greatly beloved, and instructed him to stand up because he had been sent to him. Daniel was able to get in a crawling position on hands and knees but was unable to stand.

The angel said to Daniel, "When you began to pray, God sent me to answer your prayer," see v. 12-13. The angel explained that he had been delayed. He could not get through to Daniel sooner because on the way, the prince of Persia withstood him for twenty-one days. This prince was an ambassador of Satan.

We know God has his angels organized in ranks and assignment and Satan is a great imitator of God. This unnamed angel had to send for reinforcements and that is when Michael, the archangel, had to come open up the way for him.

Hindrance Explained

Why was the way blocked? The demonic influence over Persia did not want the Jewish people free from Persian control. Satan and his forces are hindering spirits. The prince of Persia is the demon or principality assigned to the nation of Persia. Remember Daniel was held captive in Persia. Since the angel Gabriel appeared to Daniel earlier in this book, many believe that this unnamed angel was once again Gabriel.

Why was Michael called? There was a huge heavenly conflict going on involving the demonic prince of Persia and the heavenly forces who were needed to help. Michael is an archangel - a high ranking angel and he came to assist. His very name has "el" on the end, which is "God", and Michael means "who is like our God". Of course, no one is like our God. He cannot be imitated or copied.

Ephesians 6:12 explains that princes are assigned to earthly empires. Any prince opposing God is a demon prince. Hebrews 1:14 states that ministering spirits (angels) are sent forth to minister for those who will inherit salvation. So when God sends angels to help us, Satan employs his angels against the plans of God.

Daniel's prayers were delayed but not denied. Michael is the archangel in the Bible who is the watcher, the guardian and the protector of Israel. So, when Daniel interceded for Israel, Michael was sent from God to help. Michael is called "your prince" in Daniel 12:1, meaning Israel's prince. He is also mentioned in Revelation 12.

What does the Bible say about Satan? Satan is discussed in the Bible as:

• His fall –Isaiah 14:12-14
• His work-Luke 4:1-3, 5-7,9
• His agents-Luke 8:30
• His power-Job 1;14-16, Luke 13:16, 2 Cor. 11:14, Acts 5:3
• His doom- Revelation 20:10

It is Satan who stirs the nations to hatred and jealousy. He unleashes the dogs of war. He accounts for the hellish holocaust of the Jews. He is the destroyer and he is the accuser of the brethren. This same prince (a demonic force over influential empires) over Persia (Iran and Iraq today) still wants to exterminate the Jews.

The vision itself will come in chapter 11. It will have an historical and prophetic fulfillment. The angel tells Daniel that he must return to Persia to continue the fight with the demonic princes of the air. When that demonic force is defeated, the Prince of Greece will come. Literally this Prince of Greece refers to Antiochus Epiphanes, the wicked and cruel leader who came from the Seleucid Empire in 167 B.C. that we have already studied.

Prophetically, this demon prince of Greece represents secular humanism, the rationalism and mental exercise which is worship of the mind. This Greek philosophy has captured Western thought and governs today. This demonic force endeavors to destroy all interest in the supernatural realm. Churches that deny the Holy Spirit's power have bowed to the influence of the prince of Greece.

This invisible war in the heavens took place because one man with a prophetic calling prayed and fasted. The struggle in this prophecy was about Israel in the last days. That same demon of Persia is still threatening Israel. The demon prince of Greece will come.

Daniel represents a life God can use wildly in the very worst of circumstances. I have a holy longing to have this kind of relationship with God. I want what Daniel had. I desire a prayer life of intimacy with God. God has plans for the universe , this earth and for us individually. So Daniel 10:12 is for us as well as Daniel.

"Do not fear, for from the first day that you set your heart to understand, and to humble yourself before your God, your words were heard; and I have come because of your words." Be strong in the faith. Like Daniel, we too can have an intimate relationship with God.

Study Guide

CHAPTER TEN • GOD'S GLORIOUS TOUCH

Introduction

As we near the end of the book of Daniel, we know this book is not intended to be a biography of the life of Daniel, revealing his exact age or lineage. It does show God's providential guidance, His miraculous intervention, His foreknowledge and mighty power. Daniel reveals that the God of heaven controls and directs the forces of nature and the history of nations. This book reveals God's plans for His servants and His people.

1. Chapters 10-12 relate the final vision given to Daniel.

Chapter 10 is _____

Chapter 11 is_____

Chapter 12 is_____

2. This vision came to Daniel after King Cyrus had been on the throne _____ year.

3. The time of this vision was to be in the
    very near or **very distant** future. (circle one)

4. Daniel's vision took place on what day and in what month?_____
_____

5. This was just following what feast?_____

6. While Passover represented salvation through the blood, the feast of unleavened bread portrays the _____.

7. Notice Daniel extended this behavior for three more weeks. Why?_____
_____

_____

8. Even though Cyrus had been on the throne three years, he had allowed the Jews to go home to Jerusalem two years earlier. What is unusual about that?_____
_____

_____

9. Explain what happened to Daniel as he stood on the banks of the Tigris and saw a glorious vision. _____
_____

_____

_____

10. How is this description similar to what happened to the Apostle John in Revelation 1?_____
_____

_____

11. Who was the "certain man" clothed in linen and how was he dressed? _____

12. Describe Daniel falling out in the spirit. _____

_____

13. Has this experience ever happened to you? Explain.
What were the results of this experience? _____

_____

_____

_____

When the angel touched Daniel, he gained enough strength to crawl on all fours in a reverential posture, bowing low. His whole body shook and trembled.

14. Why was the angel delayed from coming to Daniel and who helped him?_____

_____

Notice that warfare broke out in Heaven because one man with a prophetic calling prayed and fasted! Who is this Prince of Persia? This strong demonic presence is the same one that is behind Islam and threatens Israel today.

Who is the prince of Greece? This is the Greek philosophy that has captured and governs Western thought. This rationalism denies the supernatural and has taken over the educational system. This prince of Greece bows to the mind of man while the prince of Persia bows to a demon god.

15. How did the angel minister to Daniel? _____ _____

_____

_____

16. Three times in the New Testament Jesus referred to Satan as the prince of this world. Paraphrase each scripture.

John 12:31_____

_____

_____

John 14:30_____

_____

_____

John 16:11_____

_____

When we go down in humility, God comes closer and lifts us up. Daniel's answer to his prayers were delayed but not denied. Read Ephesians 6:12.

17. Who is Michael? _____

• He is the archangel in the Bible   • The watcher of Israel
• Revelation 12   • Warred with Satan
• Cast Satan out of heaven   • Threw Satan to the earth
Satan's Account in Scripture:
• His Fall - Isaiah 14:12-14
• His Work- Luke 4:1-3,5-7,9
• His Agents - Luke 8:30
• His Power - Job 1:14-16, 2:7, Luke 13:16, 2 Corinthians 11:14, Acts 5:3

• His Doom - Revelation 20:10

Satan has his evil princes assigned to various nations on earth and they are well organized.

18. Read Daniel 10:15-17 and notice that Daniel fell to the ground again. What divine ministry did he receive? _____
_____

Notice that Gabriel and Michael are commissioned to protect Israel against demonic attacks. Defeating the enemy is not a one time battle. He comes in with a counterfeit of the things of God.

19. How does Revelation tell us we can defeat the enemy?_____
_____
_____
_____

20. It is amazing that God trusts Daniel with the secret mysteries of the Most High. Why?_____
_____
_____
_____

Chapter Eleven

Political Powers Unfolding

The spirit that I have seen may be a devil;
and the devil hath power to assume a pleasing shape.

William Shakespeare
Hamlet

Daniel's vision is the focus of Chapter 11. God is giving him an amplification of detail revealing the full vision, not just symbolic animals and creatures as before. I am reminded of the classic story of Macbeth at the witches' cave where he saw king after king in succession before him. Similarly through this heaven-sent vision, Daniel is permitted to see king after king appearing on the stage of history, arrogantly playing his part and making way for his successor. This is a long chapter and more difficult to understand than the others. But we will explore it carefully and decipher its important lessons.

Daniel saw in a vision a war between kings who ruled in the South and the North.

The obvious question here is south of what and north of what? This battle zone is south of the people of God and north of the people of God. Israel is the target in the middle of the wars between the Kingdoms of the North (Syria) and the Kingdoms of the South (Egypt).

This vision gives an accurate and detailed account of 125 years of history that occurred after the death of Daniel. At the end of the chapter, Israel once again is the target of the final Antichrist who is yet to come.

Israel was a buffer state between the North and the South. The covenant land and the covenant people were a doormat to

Egypt and Syria. Both sides trampled Israel underfoot. It appears that Israel's position politically may have come full circle with history trying to repeat itself.

In Daniel 11:2, this bold prophet declared "Now I tell you the truth." When the Holy Scripture speaks of history, it is accurate. When the Bible speaks geographically, scientifically, socially, morally or prophetically, the Bible speaks truth. Remember that man writes history after it happens, and God gives prophecy before it happens. In chapter 11 of Daniel, verses 2-35 have been fulfilled so they are now history and accurate! Events discussed in verses 36-45 are prophecy and will be fulfilled in the future.

In January of 2011, an uprising in Egypt calling for new leadership began to put weighty pressure upon the security of Israel. This situation appears to be taken from the pages of scripture and is a foreshadowing of the ultimate uprising that is prophesied in scripture. The confusion and division simply reflect an attitude in The Middle East that will make democracy impossible and will set the stage for a very strong dictator, possibly preparing for the Antichrist. (See Appendix.)

History Unpacked • Daniel 11:2-35

As we prepare for this study, you need to understand that the kings from north or the kings from south cannot and will never usher in peace on earth or a Utopia on this planet. Only the Lord Jesus Christ can and will do that when he comes again. Mark 13 and Matthew 24:6-8 warn us, "You will hear of wars and rumors of wars, but see to it that you are not alarmed. Such things must happen, but the end is not yet come. There will be famines and earthquakes in various places. All these are the beginning of birth pains."

It doesn't matter if we look to the north or the south, to the present or the future, the story is that nation rises against nation and nations fall with blood, panic and tears. In Daniel 11:2, Persia and Greece are mentioned by name. Egypt is named in verse 8. This chapter is full of alliances, political marriages, wars, greed, power and the sacrifice of thousands of soldiers. This prophecy concerns what we know as history, a history fulfilled in struggle between Persia, Greece, Egypt and Syria for domination of the ancient world. But the bottom line is that we can lift up our heads for our redemption draws near. Jesus is coming soon and we need to pray for His soon return.

From Ahasuerus to Antiochus • Daniel 11: 2-20

Let's look at a brief summary of the three kings that succeeded Cyrus. The three kings who appear in Persia after Cyrus are Cambyses – Son of Cyrus 529-522 B.C.; Smerdis 522-521 B.C.; and Darius Hystaspia 521-485 B.C.. The fourth one mentioned who will have far greater wealth than the others was Xerxes (Ahasuerus). He was married to Esther, the Jewish alien who took a stand for her God and was used to spare the Jews from genocide at the hand of Haman. (If you would like to study more on the life of Esther, my book, *Esther: Wrongs Made Right* contains a complete study of her life and strong courage in the face of difficulty. It is available at www.ronphillips.org.)

Xerxes attempted to invade Greece but he was defeated miserably at the Battle of Thermapoly and the Battle of Salamis, which resulted in the downfall of Persia. The mighty King who appeared out of Greece was Alexander the Great. According to Dan 11:4 at his death the empire would be broken up in four divisions. "...His empire will be broken up and parceled out toward the four winds of heaven. It will not go to his descendants, nor will it have the power he exercised, because his empire will be uprooted and given to others." (NIV)

(5) Also the king of the South shall become strong, as well as one of his princes; and he shall gain power over him and have dominion. His dominion shall be a great dominion.

(6) And at the end of some years they shall join forces, for the daughter of the king of the South shall go to the king of the North to make an agreement; but she shall not retain the power of her authority, and neither he nor his authority shall stand; but she shall be given up, with those who brought her, and with him who begot her, and with him who strengthened her in those times.

(7) But from a branch of her roots one shall arise in his place, who shall come with an army, enter the fortress of the king of the North, and deal with them and prevail.

(8) And he shall also carry their gods captive to Egypt, with their princes and their precious articles of silver and gold; and he shall continue more years than the king of the North.

(9) Also the king of the North shall come to the kingdom of the king of the South, but shall return to his own land.

(10) However his sons shall stir up strife, and assemble a multitude of great forces; and one shall certainly come and overwhelm and pass through; then he shall return to his fortress and stir up strife.

(11) And the king of the South shall be moved with rage, and go out and fight with him, with the king of the North, who shall muster a great multitude; but the multitude shall be given into the hand of his enemy.

(12) When he has taken away the multitude, his heart will be lifted up; and he will cast down tens of thousands, but he will not prevail.

(13) For the king of the North will return and muster a multitude greater than the former, and shall certainly come at the end of some years with a great army and much equipment.

(14) Now in those times many shall rise up against the king of the South. Also, violent men of your people shall exalt themselves in fulfillment of the vision, but they shall fall.

(15) So the king of the North shall come and build a siege mound, and take a fortified city; and the forces of the South shall not withstand him. Even his choice troops shall have no strength to resist.

(16) But he who comes against him shall do according to his own will, and no one shall stand against him. He shall stand in the Glorious Land with destruction in his power.

(17) He shall also set his face to enter with the strength of his whole kingdom, and upright ones with him; thus shall he do. And he shall give him the daughter of women to destroy it; but she shall not stand with him, or be for him.

(18) After this he shall turn his face to the coastlands, and shall take many. But a ruler shall bring the reproach against them to an end; and with the reproach removed, he shall turn back on him.

(19) Then he shall turn his face toward the fortress of his own land; but he shall stumble and fall, and not be found.

- Daniel 11:5-19

At the death of Alexander the Great, there was no successor so his four generals divided the kingdoms:

- Cassander
- Lysimachus
- Ptolemy Soter – Egypt which is Kingdom of South
- Seleucis – Syria which is Kingdom of North

The King of Egypt grew stronger and the King of Syria also gained strength. The daughter of the King of Egypt was Bernice who was given in marriage to the King of North. When Bernice's father died, her husband Antiochus II threw her out and reclaimed his former wife, Laodice, and their two sons. Out of hatred Laodice poisoned her husband. Antiochus then had Bernice and her young son killed.

Verse 7 reveals that Bernice (of Egypt) was survived by one brother who was outraged at his sister's death. He warred against and overthrew Syria and killed Laodice. Bernice's brother carried back to Egypt massive amounts of gold, silver and idols from Syria.

Laodice's son, Seleucus Callinicus, ruled in the North during this atrocity. To get revenge and to reclaim the wealth of Syria in 240 B.C., he planned to invade Egypt. He returned home in defeat because his fleet of ships perished in a storm. This was a fulfillment of verse 10.

The sons mentioned were the sons of Seleucus Callinicus. They were stirred up because of their father's defeat and humiliation. There were many struggles between the Ptolemies and the Seleucids until the appearance of Antiochus Epiphanes. These wars brought great suffering to the people of God and it would be many days before God's people could be a nation again. Daniel's vision is now reported in our history books.

From Antiochus Epiphanes to the Anticipation of Antichrist • Daniel 11:21-35

Antiochus Epiphanes was 8th in line of the Seleucus dynasty. You will remember from the study of Daniel 8:9-14, 23-26 that this Seleucids governor of Israel was Aniochus Epiphanes. He was a horribly wicked ruler called the mad man of the East. He came to the throne in 174 B.C. This leader is the contemptible person who seizes the kingdom through intrigue (v.21). Antiochus failed in his third invasion of Egypt because of Rome's nautical intervention. He then turned his whole fury on Palestine. He invaded Jerusalem on the Sabbath. He destroyed books of the Old Testament, forbade all Jewish worship observances and offered a sow on the holy altar of the Temple. In verses 28-31 Antiochus railed against the holy covenant and the people of God. He desecrated the temple fortress and used brute force against them. He abolished the daily sacrifices and tore down buildings of worship. He committed the abomination that causes desolation which was idol worship in the Holy Temple.

Verse 34 says "when they fall, they will receive a little help," referring to Judas Maccabaeus who was successful in bringing down Antiochus Epiphanes on December 25,165 B.C. The people firmly resisted this "madman" Antiochus in every way.

Antiochus Epiphanes came to the end of his time as all do. He was on the battlefield and struck with a raging strange disease. In a very short time, he died. He was gone and so was his contemptible hatred of God's people.

Prophecy Foretold • When Antichrist Comes

He will lash out against the holy covenant. He will favor, entice and give consent to those who abandon and deny the faith. Sadly, there will be traitors who walk away.

He will desecrate the temple fortress when his campaign for absolute control has run its course. If he cannot get his way through treaties, flattery or deceit, Antichrist will use brute force.

He will abolish the daily sacrifices. Public worship will be denied – impossible – illegal. No praise, worship, preaching or thanksgiving allowed. Church buildings will be torn down or will become museums, government buildings, etc. Instead of worshipping Jehovah God, idol worship will be the norm. This is "abomination that causes desolation."

What are the people of God to do in persecution? Believers have tools to fight off the evil ones! The way we resist is to live for Christ, walk daily with Him, and utilize prayer, worship and devotion to God as Daniel demonstrated with his life.

From Antichrist to Armageddon • Daniel 11:36-45

(36) Then the king shall do according to his own will: he shall exalt and magnify himself above every god, shall speak blasphemies against the God of gods, and shall prosper till the wrath has been accomplished; for what has been determined shall be done.

(37) He shall regard neither the God of his fathers nor the desire of women, nor regard any god; for he shall exalt himself above them all.

(38) But in their place he shall honor a god of fortresses; and

a god which his fathers did not know he shall honor with gold and silver, with precious stones and pleasant things.

(39)Thus he shall act against the strongest fortresses with a foreign god, which he shall acknowledge, and advance its glory; and he shall cause them to rule over many, and divide the land for gain.

(40) At the time of the end the king of the South shall attack him; and the king of the North shall come against him like a whirlwind, with chariots, horsemen, and with many ships; and he shall enter the countries, overwhelm them, and pass through.

(41) He shall also enter the Glorious Land, and many countries shall be overthrown; but these shall escape from his hand: Edom, Moab, and the prominent people of Ammon.

(42) He shall stretch out his hand against the countries, and the land of Egypt shall not escape.

(43) He shall have power over the treasures of gold and silver, and over all the precious things of Egypt; also the Libyans and Ethiopians shall follow at his heels.

(44) But news from the east and the north shall trouble him; therefore he shall go out with great fury to destroy and annihilate many.

(45) And he shall plant the tents of his palace between the seas and the glorious holy mountain; yet he shall come to his end, and no one will help him.

- Daniel 11: 36-45

The Antichrist, much like Antiochus Epiphanes, will wade into history through a river of blood. Verses 36 to the end of the chapter refer to the man of lawlessness who is the final world dictator, the Antichrist of the Great Tribulation. Where the Lord Jesus Christ saves, the Antichrist destroys. Jesus is the Son of God and the Antichrist is the son of Satan or perdition. Jesus came to serve and Antichrist came to rule. Jesus came to bring love and peace while the Antichrist will come to bring hate and war. Jesus rules with the Word and the Spirit while Antichrist will rule with a sword and a spear. Jesus frees us from sin and Antichrist enslaves to sin.

Many Old Testament men have been types of or have been a foreshadowing of the Lord Jesus Christ. Moses, Joseph, David, Solomon, Daniel, Jonah, Joshua, Melchizedek, Abraham, Jacob and others had traits that pointed to Jesus. But there is only one in the Old Testament that is a type or foreshadowing of the Antichrist and that is Antiochus Epiphanes. The Antichrist will pretend to be God and try to defeat God by taking over God's throne on earth and abolishing worship of God. Because he hates God, he hates God's people. He has a strong desire to conquer the beautiful and glorious land of Israel which is the apple of God's eye.

For a time the Antichrist will have supremacy. Verses 36-37 explain, "Then the king shall do according to his own will: he shall exalt and magnify himself above every god, shall speak blasphemies against the God of gods, and shall prosper till the wrath has been accomplished; for what has been determined shall be done. He shall regard neither the God of his fathers nor the desire of women, nor regard any god; for he shall exalt himself above them all."

He will do whatever he desires to do. He will choose to exalt himself and magnify himself above all other gods and to speak horrible things against the God of gods. This is also in 2 Thessalonians 2:4, "He will oppose and will exalt himself over everything that is called God or is worshiped, so that he sets himself up in God's temple, proclaiming himself to be God." (NIV).

Strangely this Antichrist is the beast of Revelation 13:4, 8 who is worshipped by the whole earth.

The rule of Antichrist is the Great Tribulation. His rule is for 7 years and then God will intervene and stop the war.

"...neither shall he regard the God of his fathers..."

This Antichrist could very well be an apostate Jew as described here in Daniel 11:37. It is not feasible that anyone other than a Jew would present himself as Israel's Messiah.

"...nor the desire of women"

This phrase, also found in verse 37, may refer to the fact that Jewish women wanted to be the mother of the Messiah. This wicked one hates God, denies Jesus as the Son of God and pretends to be the promised Messiah himself.

"he honors the gods of forces,"

This phrase in verse 38 means gods of strongholds. He made his own god which fights wars and gains victories. He creates his own kind of love, which is defined by having mankind at his feet and having dominion over humanity.

Antichrist will have his headquarters set up between the Mediterranean Sea and Jerusalem. He will be destroyed by the physical return of the Lord Jesus Christ.

(17) Then I saw an angel standing in the sun; and he cried with a loud voice, saying to all the birds that fly in the midst of heaven, "Come and gather together for the supper of the great God,

(18) that you may eat the flesh of kings, the flesh of captains, the flesh of mighty men, the flesh of horses and of those who sit on them, and the flesh of all people, free and slave, both small and great."
(19) And I saw the beast, the kings of the earth, and their armies, gathered together to make war against Him who sat on the horse and against His army.
(20) Then the beast was captured, and with him the false prophet who worked signs in his presence, by which he deceived those who received the mark of the beast and those who worshiped his image. These two were cast alive into the lake of fire burning with brimstone.
- Revelation 19:17-20

Daniel spoke, saying, "I saw in my vision by night, and behold, the four winds of heaven were stirring up the Great Sea."
- Daniel 7:2

Then he said to me, "The waters which you saw, where the harlot sits, are peoples, multitudes, nations, and tongues."
- Revelation 17:15

If we are alive during the rise of this abominable Antichrist, then what are we to do?

- **Resist** him at every opportunity.
- **Refuse** to be taken in by his deceit and power.
- **Remain** faithful to the Lord Jesus Christ as his bride and his church.

Whenever the world brushes against God's people then the events are recorded in the book. Everything revolves around God's people and God's precious Holy Land of Israel.

The end of the Antichrist will be just as sudden and just as unexpected as that of Antiochus Epiphanes. Daniel 11:45 states, "He will come to his end and no one will help him." Amen.!!!

Antichrist cannot possibly win, no one prevails against the power of Almighty God, not Antichrist or Antiochus or anyone. Regardless of what Antichrist does, or how much power he accumulates, or how many people he leads astray, it is Jesus Christ who wins!

Daniel chapter 11 is in the Bible for us to know three things:

• The church, the covenant people of God, is central to world history.
• The Antichrist hates and attacks the church.
• The Antichrist's opposition to God's people will lead to his downfall.

People of God, we must suit up in the full armor of God.

Ephesians 6:10-13 instructs us, "Be strong in the Lord and in his mighty power. Put on the full armor of God so that you can take your stand against the devil's schemes. For our struggle is not against flesh and blood, but against the rulers, against the authorities, against the powers of this dark world and against the spiritual forces of evil in the heavenly realms. Therefore put on the full armor of God, so that when the day of evil comes, you may be able to stand your ground, and after you have done everything, to stand. (NIV)

Those who are armed can take their stand to oppose the evil. According to Daniel 11:32, "...The people who know their God will firmly resist him".(NIV)

The Condition of Egypt
Chapter 11 Appendix

Isaiah 19

Isaiah 19:1 says, "Behold, the Lord rides on a swift cloud and will come into Egypt." Isaiah 19:17 states, "And the land of Judah shall be a terror unto Egypt." These prophetic verses could be taking place as we watch Egypt's civil war unfold. For weeks, the economy of Egypt is at a standstill while hundreds of thousands march in the streets.

Isaiah 19:2 says, "And I will set Egyptians against Egyptians; and they shall fight everyone against his brother, and everyone against his neighbor; city against city, kingdom against kingdom". "Christ will fight Egypt because the Antichrist will occupy Egypt." says Walid Shoebat (p.227) *God's War on Terror*.

Isaiah 19:4, "And the Egyptians will I give over into the hand of a cruel lord and a fierce king shall rule over them says the Lord, the Lord of Hosts." As we studied in Daniel 11:2, "He (Antichrist) shall stretch out his hand against the countries, and the land of Egypt shall not escape."

Christ will ultimately rescue a remnant by Egypt from Antichrist. "In that day shall five cities in the land of Egypt speak the language of Canaan, and swear to the Lord of Hosts: one shall be called, the city of destruction." Isaiah 19:2-3 says many Egyptians will become like Messianic Jews and love to speak Hebrew.

My husband and I had the privilege of visiting Egypt for 14 days in April 2010. Our most enjoyable part of the trip was visiting the Cairo church led by Pastor Noor. On that Monday night, the church was packed with more than 2,000 people for a regular prayer meeting. People of several languages participated. We wore the headsets so we could understand in our own English language. How they sang, preached and prayed! I was blessed to get to pray with a woman from England and another from Australia out loud – holding hands in a Christian church! Only God would connect England, Australia and America to pray together in Cairo.

These Christian Egyptians are severely oppressed. Pastor Noor told us privately of the many times he had been arrested and his life threatened, but God overturned all plans of the evil one.

I believe these oppressed believers will be rescued by our Messiah. Isaiah 19:20 says, "And it will be for a sign and for a witness to the Lord of Hosts in the land of Egypt; for they will cry to the Lord because of their oppressors, and He will send them a Savior and a Might One, and He will deliver them."

The Egyptian Coptics are increasingly being oppressed by the Muslim majority, and even by the government. But if God sees their cause as being important enough to personally rescue them, then why are we so silent about the suffering Coptic Christians and evangelical Christians in Egypt?

Study Guide

CHAPTER ELEVEN • POLITICAL POWERS UNFOLDING

Introduction

Remember that Daniel 10-12 is all the same vision. Chapter 11 is of monumental importance to the encouragement of God's people and that is the reason Satan's forces hindered the angel of God from coming immediately to Daniel in chapter 10.

The answer to Daniel's prayer is a prophecy concerning two nations which were of foremost importance in relation to Daniel's people. In this very difficult chapter we see divisions which separate history and prophecy—the historical and the eschatological section.

This prophecy bridges the gap from Media-Persia to Greece, from Asia to Europe, and reveals world powers transposing from one continent to another, East to West.

1. The speaker in this chapter is still the _____ of chapter 10.

2. Daniel **did** or **did not** live to see the fulfillment of this prophecy? (circle one)

3. Why do you think this vision was recorded in Holy Scripture?

_____

_____

_____

Daniel 11:4 refers to the Kings of Persia (or the Kings of the North).

The King	Ruled
Cambyses	529 B.C.
Pseudo-Smerdis	522 B.C.
Darius Hystaspia	521-485 B.C.
Xerxes (richest)	485- 465 B.C. Invaded Greece but failed.

4. What do you already know about Xerxes (Ahasuerus)? _____

_____

_____

_____

5. Who is the "mighty King" who came to power in 335 B.C. and assumed world dominion? _____

6. In review, the Grecian Empire broke into 4 parts after the death of Alexander the Great. Name and identify each one of the rulers.

Name	Area	Direction
Cassandra	_____	_____
Lepimachus	_____	_____
Ptolemy	_____	_____
Seleucus	_____	_____

Read verses 21-25 about Antiochus Epiphanes, the 8th ruler in the Seleucid Dynasty who was horribly evil.

Notice in these verses that this dynasty is from the Kings of the North and it will help you organize your thoughts:

Daniel 11:5   Seleucus I Nicator (312-281 B.C.)
No reference   Antiochus I Soter (281-262 B.C.)
Daniel 11:6   Antiochus II Theos (262-246 B.C.)
Daniel 11:7-9   Seleucus II Callinicus (246-227 B.C.)
Daniel 11:10   Selucus III Sorter (227-223B.C.)
Daniel 11:10-11,
13, 15-19   Antiochus III the Great (223-197 B.C.)
Daniel 11:20   Seleucus IV Philopater (187-176 B.C.)
Daniel 11:21-32   Antiochus Epiphanes (175-163 B.C.)
                    (Beth Moore study of Daniel p. 215)

7. This Antiochus Epiphanes was the King of _____
and called the "little horn". He is not the _____
of the Great Tribulation but is a type or metaphor of this final
Antichrist that will come. Notice the date he came to power was

_____.

8. Describe this villain's character. _____
_____
_____
_____

9. From Daniel 11:30-31, list four things that Antiochus Epiphanes
attempted.
Verse 30_____

Verse 31_____

Verse 31 _____

Verse 31 _____

Antiochus Epiphanes will not be completely successful in his campaign against the "holy covenant" because "the people who know their God will firmly resist him."

10. Explain the death of Antiochus Epiphanes._____

_____

_____

_____

_____

11. Daniel 11:36-45 refer to the _____

The final end time _____ and the period known as

the Great _____.

12. List below the characteristics and purpose of:

The Lord Jesus Christ   **The Antichrist**

1. _____   _____

2. _____   _____

3. _____   _____

4. _____   _____

5. _____   _____

6. _____   _____

13. The Antichrist, like Antiochus Epiphanes, will not destroy the "Holy Covenant". Daniel assures us that the people who know their God will firmly resist him. What does the Antichrist want to accomplish? _____

_____

_____

_____

14. Verse 41 tells us that 2 countries, _____ and _____ will be delivered from the Antichrist's hands. These are the traditional enemies of Israel. So, the Antichrist will accept the ancient saying, "the enemy of my enemy must be my friend".

15. Where do verses 44-45 tell us the Antichrist's headquarters will be located? What will be his end? _____

_____

_____

_____

16. List 10 characters in the Old Testament who were types or a foreshadowing of the Lord Jesus Christ. For example Joseph.

1. _____   6. _____

2. _____   7. _____

3. _____   8. _____

4. _____   9. _____

5. _____   10. _____

17. Who is the only character in the Old Testament who is a type of or foreshadows the coming of the Antichrist? _____

_____

18. Paraphrase Psalm 79:1-2 _____

_____

_____

19. Paraphrase Revelation 19:17-20 _____

_____

_____

20. Paraphrase Revelation 17:15 _____

_____

_____

21. Paraphrase Daniel 7:2 _____

_____

_____

22. If we, the believers, are alive during the rise of the Antichrist what are we instructed to do?_____

_____

This Antichrist will be the worst and most cruel tyrant the world has ever known. Think of the worst tyrants from history and know that the final son of perdition will be worse than all put together and more.

Prophecy of the Seventy Weeks

Decree of Artaxerxes March 14, 445 B.C. Nehemiah 2:1-8		Presentation of Messiah April 6, 33 A.D. Triumphal Entry Luke 19:28-40	
Daniel 9:25 Sixty-Nine Weeks (483 Years)		Daniel 9:26 Gap of Time	
7 Weeks 7x7= 49 Years Complete Rebuilding of Jerusalem	62 Weeks 62x7=434 Years	Messiah cut off April 11, 33 A.D. Jerusalem and Temple Destroyed August 6, 70 A.D. Church Age begins John 1:9, 11, 12 Israel targeted wars and persecutions	

(490 Years)

	Covenant of Antichrist with Israel	Return of Christ
	Daniel 9:27 **Seventieth Week (7 Years)**	
	3.5 Years	3.5 Years	
	Antichrist covenant with Israel	Desecration by Antichrist	
	Image of Antichrist in Temple	Six purposes finished v. 24	
	Declares himself God		

Chapter Twelve

My Prince Will Come

Crossing the Bar

Sunset and evening star,
And one clear call for me!
And may there be no moaning of the bar
When I put out to sea.

But such a tide as moving seems asleep,
Too full for sound and foam,
When that which drew from out
the boundless deep turns again home.

Twilight and evening bell,
And after that the dark!
And may there be no sadness of farewell,
When I embark;

For tho' from out our bourne of Time and Place
The flood may bear me far,
I hope to see my Pilot face to face
When I have crossed the bar

Alfred Lord Tennyson

As we approach the last chapter in the book of Daniel, I hope you have a strong sense of accomplishment as this is a very difficult book to study. The Bible says we are to love the Lord our God with our hearts, souls and minds and this has been a huge exercise of our minds.

The title of this chapter is "My Prince will Come". Even though the end time 7-year tribulation will be the worst possible time the world has ever known, our God still has it covered. He will end it all and His excellent plan will be accomplished on earth as it is in heaven. God's son will come and save us. The son of the Most High God will come to bring swift judgment on the Antichrist and the false prophet. The Prince of all Princes, Jesus, will set up the millennial reign on the earth and the eternal reign in heaven.

I am reminded of the fairy tale Snow White. While this young girl was tormented, mistreated and emotionally battered by her wicked and horrible stepmother, she kept her song. She maintained her optimistic and cheerful attitude. Even when this hateful and wicked woman tried to poison her with an enticing red apple, she endured the pain and near death experience. She had longed for her prince to come and he did. He saved her and gave her a new life full of romance and provision. And as most fairy tales end, they lived happily ever after.

The book of Daniel is no fairy tale–it is absolute and accurate prophecy, much of which is already fulfilled. However, we like Snow White will endure many attacks, mistreatments and pitfalls-- but our prince will come. The Prince of all Princes, the Lord Jesus Christ, will deliver us, save us, and give us a new life with Him in the millennium.

Remember, the first 6 chapters of Daniel are all about the times of the Gentiles. In chapter 2 we read about the beginning of the Gentile power with the head of the statue representing Babylon as the head of gold but concluding with the stone who is the Lord Jesus Christ smashing the statue.

The last six chapters are all about the future plan for Israel-Daniel's people. In chapter 7 we read about the vision which begins part way through the statue of nations and ends with the kingdom being given to Christ (7:13-14) and his saints (7:27).

Chapter 8 shows us the last emperor that will rule in the early Grecian Empire and ends with him being broken by the Prince of Princes.

In chapter 9 we learn of the decree to rebuild Jerusalem and the crucifixion of Christ (9:25-26). This prophecy ends with the judgments on both Antichrist and Israel, and the second coming of Christ.

Chapters 10-12 are all one unit and one full vision. In chapter 11 we study both Persian and Grecian history and the Antichrist rise to the appointed time for the tribulation for Israel.

In chapter 12 we read the grand finale of all the preceding visions and it brings us once again to the end of the times of the Gentiles and the end of the tribulation period.

Chapter 12 begins with "at this time". The future is addressed to "thy" people or Israel. Daniel knows for sure that he will die and not see the first or the second coming of Christ, but will be raised at the millennium to reign with our Lord.

This entire book has been about literal kingdoms on this earth. All of the dreams and visions have portrayed literal king-doms that have come and gone exactly as the Lord revealed to Daniel. We saw the rise and fall of the Babylonian Empire, the Medes and the Persians, the Grecian Empire, the four empires from Alexander the Great and we even studied the Roman Empire.

That being true, we must believe that the Millennial Reign of Christ is also a literal kingdom set up on this earth and that is what this book has been leading up to for eleven chapters. Everything before chapter 12 points to the kingdom that God will set up for his saints who will reign with him here on earth.

The Tribulation

(1) At that time Michael shall stand up, the great prince who stands watch over the sons of your people; and there shall be a time of trouble, such as never was since there was a nation, even to that time. And at that time your people shall be deliv-ered, every one who is found written in the book.
(2) And many of those who sleep in the dust of the earth shall awake, some to everlasting life, some to shame and everlast-ing contempt.
- Daniel 12:1-2

The twentieth century has been a century of wars from WWI, WWII, Korea, The Cold War, Vietnam, Desert Storm, Iraq, Afghanistan and we continue to be at war. The coming Tribulation will be much worse than this, a time of trouble such as never pre-viously was seen on the earth.

Matthew 24:21 tells us the nation of Israel can expect great misery and horror before Messiah returns, "For then there will be great tribulation, such as has not been since the beginning of the world until this time, no, nor ever shall be."

This will happen directly before the Son of Man comes to earth in power and great glory. There will be wars in heaven and Michael and the angels shall fight against the dragon (Satan). Satan will carry out his hellish design against the Jewish people. Israel will "pass under the rod" as described in Ezekiel 20:34-38. In Ezekiel 22:18-22 we learn they will pass through the furnace of affliction. The woman of revelation is the remnant of Israel who will be the main target of Satan's vengeance.

The Tribulation will begin with the contract signed by Antichrist and Israel. They will become great friends. Antichrist will even build the Jewish temple. But it is all a ruse to manipulate Israel.

Three and one half years into the tribulation, Antichrist will walk into the temple and declare himself god and demand to be worshipped just as Nebuchadnezzar did in chapter 3. Israel's eyes will be opened and they will refuse to submit to this son of perdition. The last three and one-half years will be the Great Tribulation, for persecution will be extreme and many will be martyred.

At this time a remnant of Israel is preserved (the "elect" of Israel spoken of in Matthew 24:22 are the 144,000). These Jews will be martyred and resurrected for the millennial reign. (Isaiah 11:1, 27:12-13, Jeremiah 30:7, Ezekiel 37:21-28, Hosea 3:4-5 and Amos 9:11-15)

The Truth • Daniel 12:3-4

During this darkest period of history, God will have His light bearers on the earth to live wisely and instruct in righteousness. When existence is unbearable a great revival will take place. People will be running here and there and knowledge will increase. That is very understandable in this information age.

When we visited Egypt, we saw on every home, apartment building and little shanty hovels along the river a satellite dish on the rooftops. Even these remote mud houses are connected to the rest of the world. We are connected globally with all kinds of technology. As the end times approach, the book of Daniel which has been sealed up will be sought out, studied and proclaimed.

The Time • Daniel 12:5-7

The specifics of the vision are most difficult. The place of the vision is the Tigris River which is also mentioned in Daniel 10:4. The man clothed in linen is the same one as mentioned in chapter 10. In addition to the angel who was announced in verse one, two other angels appear, each one standing on opposite sides of the river. The man in linen is enormous and hovers over the top of the waters. The two angels may represent what the scripture says in 2 Corinthians 13:1, "...By the mouth of two or three witnesses every word shall be established.". I believe the man in linen is the Lord Jesus Christ who speaks to answer Daniel's question, "How long will this take until the end?"

The Lord says in verse 7, "time, times, and a half time" which we have learned previously is 3.5 years. In verse 7 our Lord holds up his right hand and holds up his left hand and swears by Him who lives forever.

God gives this promise in Ezekiel 20:5-6, "Say to them, 'Thus says the Lord God: "On the day when I chose Israel and raised My hand in an oath to the descendants of the house of Jacob, and made Myself known to them in the land of Egypt, I raised My hand in an oath to them, saying, 'I am the Lord your God.' On that day I raised My hand in an oath to them, to bring them out of the land of Egypt into a land that I had searched out for them, 'flowing with milk and honey,' the glory of all lands.

God raised his hand in an oath saying "I Am the Lord your God". He repeats that oath in verses 7, 9, 15, and 19. But in Daniel our Lord lifts both hands in an oath. This is doubly important. He swears using both hands which is over the top emphatic.

Make no mistake about it, God is emphasizing His promise that when the time is up, He will deliver His people. Let me remind you that this is the 1,260 days of Revelation 11:3 (Jewish calendar 360 day year) and the same as the 42 months in Revelation 13:5.

In this last half of the Tribulation, God, through the Antichrist, will accomplish His judgment on Israel. Then Messiah will come and the nations will humble themselves, repent of their sins and acknowledge Christ as Lord of Lords, King of Kings and Savior of all mankind.

Many will repent and come to Christ but according to Revelation 22:11, 12, "He that is unjust, let him be unjust still, he which is filthy let him be filthy still." Not all people will repent. Many will repent but many will still want to be their own god and refuse to yield to Jehovah God.

In Daniel 12:11-12 we see the Tribulation or the 70 weeks of years and two new numbers, 1,290 days, which is 30 days more than the 3.5 years stated earlier. In verse 12 we read 1,335 days.

Commentaries vary on what these numbers represent. The extra days could be for the clean up, purifying and preparing the way for the millennial reign. Also this time could be the time of judgments for the living, as mentioned in Matthew 25: 31-46.

Daniel heard but he did not understand. He cried, "Lord, what shall be the end of these things?" Daniel wanted to know how it all would end and so do we. God did not give the answer to Daniel but told him there was no need to probe any further. At the appointed time, God would bring everything to pass just as the vision stated.

In verse 10 the reference is that those who go through the tribulation will come out of the purging purified and in blood washed garments of white. When God chastens His children, it is always for their profit and purification. Hebrews 12:10 gives the contrast between parental correction and God's correction, "They disciplined us for a little while as they thought best; but God disciplines us for our good, in order that we may share in his holiness."

In the Great Tribulation Jews will be saved (Revelation 7:13-14). The apostle Paul said in 1 Corinthians 2:9-10, "But as it is written, eye hath not seen, nor ear heard, neither has entered into the heart of man, the things which God hath prepared for them that love him. But God has revealed them unto us by His Spirit; for the spirit searches all things, yes, the deep things of God. "

The secret things belong to God but when they are revealed they are for the believers, their children and generations to come. Daniel knew he had been given a great mystery to hold on to.

In verse 13 God tells Daniel to rest. Daniel had been taken into captivity when he was around 15 years of age. He lived through the 70 years of the Jewish captivity. Now he has heard instructions to go and rest. He had survived toil, trouble, disappointments and now they were all over.

He had a strange yet wonderful journey and it was about to end on this earth. No longer the target for cruel and jealous men, Daniel had seen his last den of hungry lions. He was a good man, full of God and faithful. Daniel was tested yet true. He was loving and loyal to his God.

Daniel never failed to fast, pray and be fearless before others. He had the reassurance that in the future he would rise from the dead to enter the millennium. For Daniel, there was rest, resurrection and reward waiting for him. This is true for all of us as well. Revelation 14:13 states "blessed are the dead which die in the Lord…they shall rest from their labors; and their works do follow them". Amen.

The book of Daniel comes to an end with this victorious promise, one day our Prince will come!

Maranatha was the early Christian greeting instead of hello or good-bye. It is Greek for "the Lord is coming soon." So let us diligently devote all the strength we have to reach our family, friends, and acquaintances with the Gospel. The time is short.

Maranatha!

Study Guide

CHAPTER TWELVE • OUR PRINCE WILL COME

Introduction

In this epilogue we learn that, like Daniel, we should "go our way" in witness and service to our Lord until the end when we stand before Him. There is so much we will never know, but we can rest assured that a glorious inheritance is waiting for us, (Daniel 12:13).

1. Read Revelation 20 which is about the end of the prophetic timeline. What happens in this account?_____

_____

_____

_____

_____

_____

2. What will happen to the beast and false prophet?_____

_____

_____

_____

3. What will happen to the people who refuse to receive the beast's mark? How will it be done?_____

_____

_____

4. Where is Daniel in Chapter 12?_____

5. Whom are with him?_____

_____

6. What are some other phrases used for the Great Tribulation?

_____

_____

_____

_____

_____

- Read Matthew 24:21
- Read Ezekiel 20:34-38
- Read Ezekiel 22:18-22

7. What will be the triumph of the Jews in Daniel 12:2?

_____

_____

_____

- Read Matthew 24:22
- Read Isaiah 1:1, 27:12-13, Jeremiah 30:7, Ezekiel 37:21-18
- Read Hosea 3:4-5

• Read Amos 9:11-15

8. What is the time of the end? How does that correspond to what we already know? _____

_____

_____

_____

9. Read and paraphrase 1 Corinthians 2:9-10. _____

_____

_____

_____

_____

10. What have you learned from your study of Daniel?_____

_____

_____

_____

11. What has blessed you the most?_____

_____

_____

12. We live in difficult times and the future will hold a time of trouble such as never was before. Where will the Christians be during the tribulation? _____

_____

_____

Signs of the Times
Chapter 12 Appendix

*And they will fall by the edge of the sword, and be led away
captive into all nations. And Jerusalem will be trampled by
Gentiles until the times of the Gentiles are fulfilled.*
- Luke 21:24

Sign #1 – Israel is the timepiece to determine what is going on
with end times. Jews will be killed and Jerusalem will be controlled by non-Jews.

Sign #2 – The desperation of Nations will occur in Luke 21. The
rise of Islam and a false peace will disturb nations. Jerusalem itself
will be split as Revelation 6:1 states.

Sign #3 – Convulsions of nature like Hurricane Katrina that hit
New Orleans, the volcano that erupted in Iceland, Tsunamis', the
Chilean earthquake will be consuming. We are aware of sunspots
that have the potential to stop all communication systems on
earth. That would include cell phones, check cards, cable communications which could cause enormous stress to families,
economies, and world politics. Nature will be out of order as
Matthew 24 states.

Sign #4 – Demonic disruptions in the heavenlies and the prince
of the power of the air will disturb and discredit foundations of
faith.

Sign #5 – Luke 17 states that people will be preoccupied with busy, overactive schedules just as they were in the days of Noah.

Sign #6 – Ezekiel 16 states that like in the days of Lot, people will live together without the benefit of marriage, perversion and homosexuality will be rampant, idleness and abominations will be commonplace and fullness of bread will be the focus.

Sign #7 –Wars over Jerusalem took place in 1952, 1967, 1973 and continue today. Luke 21 states that when we see all these things happening, we should look up for our redemption is drawing very near.

End Time Happenings
Chapter 12 Appendix

Outline of Seal, Trumpet and Bowl Judgments

A. Seal Judgments
   1. 1st through 4th Seal Judgments: Four horsemen
      a. White Horse: Antichrist (6:1-2)
      b. Red Horse: WWIII (6:3-4)
      c. Black Horse: World depression except rich (6:5-6)
      d. Pale Green Horse: One-fourth of world dies (6:7-8)
   2. 5th Seal Judgment: Martyred souls under the altar (6:9-11)
   3. 6th Seal Judgment: Great earthquake (6:12-17)
   4. 7th Seal Judgment: Is the 7 Trumpet Judgments with a great earthquake (8:1-2)

B. Seven Trumpet Judgments (8:2; 11:19)
   1. 1st Trumpet: Hail and fire mixed with blood, thrown to earth, 1/3 of earth set on fire. 1/3 of trees burned and all grass burned. (8:7)
   2. 2nd Trumpet: Great mountain of fire thrown into sea. 1/3 of water in sea becomes blood, 1/3 of all things living in sea died. 1/3 of all ships on sea were destroyed. (8:8-9)
   3. 3rd Trumpet: Great flaming star fell out of sky, burning like a torch. Falling on 1/3 of rivers and on springs of water. The name of the star was Bitterness. Making 1/3 of water bitter and many people died because the water was so bitter. (8:10)
   4. 4th Trumpet: One-third of sun was struck and 1/3 of moon and 1/3 of stars and they became dark. 1/3 of the day was dark and 1/3 of the night also (8:12)

5. Eagle cries out over world, "Terror, terror, terror to all who belong to this world because of what will happen when the last three angels blow their trumpets." (8:13)

6. 5th Trumpet and 1st Terror: Fallen star (angel) given key to bottomless pit and releases locust with power to sting like scorpions. They were not to hurt the vegetation or anyone with the seal of God. They were not to kill them but to torture them for five months with agony like the pain of scorpion stings. (9:1-12).

7. 6th Trumpet and 2nd Terror: Release of four (fallen) angels who are bound at Euphrates River. They looked like horses with riders sitting on them. They kill 1/3 of all the people on earth with fire, smoke and burning sulfur that came from the mounts of the horses (9:13-21)

8. 7th Trumpet is the 3rd Terror and the 7 Bowl Judgments (11:15-19)

C. Seven Bowl Judgments

1. 1st Bowl Judgment: Malignant sores broke out on everyone who had the mark of the beast and who worshipped his statue. (16:2)

2. 2nd Bowl Judgment: Sea becomes like the blood of a corpse. Everything in the sea dies. (16:3)

3. 3rd Bowl Judgment: Rivers and springs become blood. (16:4)

4. 4th Bowl Judgment: Sun scorches everyone with its fire. (16:8)

5. 5th Bowl Judgment: The throne of the beast and his kingdom are plunged into darkness. (16:10)

6. 6th Bowl Judgment: Euphrates River is dried up allowing kings from the east to march westward. (16:12)

7. Three evil spirits that looked like frogs leap from the mouth

of the dragon, the beast, and the false prophet. These miracle-working demons caused all the rulers of the world to gather for battle against the Lord on that great judgment day of God Almighty. (16:13-14)

8. 7th Bowl Judgment: Mighty shout came from the throne of the Temple in heaven, saying, "It is finished!" and there was an earthquake greater than ever before in human history. Babylon split into three pieces and cities around the world destroyed. Every island disappeared and all the mountains were leveled. Hailstones weighing seventy-five pounds fell from the sky onto the people (16:17-20).

BIBLIOGRAPHY

Campbell, Daniel: Decoder of Dreams, Victor Books,
    Wheaton, Illinois. 1981

Chris@DrZimmerman.com   www.daily-scriptures.org

DeHaan, M. R. M.D. Daniel The Prophet. Lamplighter Books Grand
    Rapids, Michigan. Zondervan Publishing House. 1975

Greene, Oliver B. Daniel. The Gospel House. Inc., Greenville, South
    Carolina. 1969

Heslop, William G. D.D. Diamonds From Daniel.
    Kregel Publications. Grand Rapids, Michigan. 1979

Holy Bible. New King James Version.

Larkin, Rev. Clarence. The Book of Daniel. Published by Clarence
    Larkin. 1929

Leupold, H.D. The Exposition of Daniel. Baker Book House, Grand
    Rapids, Michigan. 1969

Luck, G. Coleman. Daniel. Moody Press, Chicago. 1958

McClain, Alva. J. Dr. Daniel's Prophecy of the 70 Weeks. Academie
    Books, Zondervan Publishing House, Grand Rapids, Michigan.
    1969

Miller, Stephen R. The New American Commentary – Daniel
Vol. 18 Broadman and Holman Publishers. USA 1977

Moore, Beth. Daniel Lives of Integrity/Words of Prophecy. Lifeway
Press, Nashville, TN. 2006

Phillips, Ron. M. D.M sermon notes on the book of Daniel.
Unpublished.

Porteous, Narman W. Daniel A Commentary.
The Westminster Press, Philadelphia, PA 1965

Strauss, Lehman, The Prophecies of Daniel, Loizeaux Brothers,
Neptune, New Jersey. 1969

Thieme, R.B. Jr. Daniel (chapters one through six pamphlets)
Berachah Tapes And Publications, Houston, TX 1973

Wilson, Robert Dick, Ph.D., D. D. Studies in the Book of Daniel,
Vol. 1, Baker Book House, Grand Rapids, Michigan. 1972

Wilson, Robert Dick., Ph.D., D.D. Studies in the Book of Daniel,
(new paperback One volume edition) Vol. 1
Baker Book House, Grand Rapids, Michigan. 1979

Young, Edward J. Th.M., Ph.D. The Prophecy of Daniel A
Commentary. WM.B

Eerdmans Publishing Co. Grand Rapids, Michigan 1975

Anderson, Sir Robert, K.C.B., L.L.D. The Coming Prince.
    14th Edition. Kregel Publications, Grand Rapids, Mi. c. 1957

Phillips, John. Exploring The Book of Daniel.
    Kregal Publications Inc. Grand Rapids, Mi. c. 2004

Shoebat, Walid and Joel Richardson. God's War on Terror

(Islam, Prophecy and The Bible) c., 2008 Top Executive Media

Willmington, Dr. H.L. Willmington's Guide to the Bible,
    Tyndale House Publishers, Wheaton, Illinois. c. 1983 - p. 228

Study Guide Answer Key

Chapter One • Life Interrupted

1. Nebuchadnezzar, Jehoikam

2. They worshipped false gods and abandoned the one true God

3. 605 BC - Daniel, Hananiah, Mishael, Azariah carried off to Babylon by Nebuchadnezzar
598 BC - Jehoikim dead. Ezekiel and sacred temple vessels carried to Babylon
587 BC - Zedikiah taken to Babylon. Holocaust of Jerusalem, city burned, temple leveled

4. Shinar, Babel, Chaldea, Ur

5. Daniel Lived in Judea-Jerusalem-privileged, brilliant, handsome, aristocracy- perhaps royal family, knew the scriptures, heard Ezekiel and Jeremiah preach

6. Aramaic Chapters 2:4b-7:28-world information and future history
Hebrew Chapters 1:1-24, 8:1-12:13 pertains only to them

7. A prophet represented God to the people of Israel
Daniel's gift of prophecy delivered to pagan and heathen court and gentile world

8. God is my Judge, Beltshazzar, prince of God
Yahweh is gracious, Shadrach, sun god
Who is like God is,   Meshach, like shack(Ishtar)

Yahweh has helped, Abednego, servant of Nego

9. Beloved, precious

10.

11.

12.

13.

14. Babylonian culture, literature, assimilate them to lose their Jewish Identity.

15. Purpose-decide. He resolved not to defile himself with food or wine from the King's table and God honored him with better health and made him 10 times smarter than all the men of Babylon.

16. It was unclean under Jewish Law. To share a meal is to commit to friendship. Meat and wine that had been offered to idols was always a toast to the gods of Babylon

17. Great health and 10 times smarter

18. Being the same person all the time, "no costume changes"

19.

20.

21.

22. True

23.

24.

25. No

26.

27.

Chapter Two • When Government Goes Bad

1. He gave them the interpretation of the dream

2.

3.

4.

5. He bowed and worshipped Daniel

6. Many great gifts, Postion of ruler in the kingdom

7. Red Sea Crossing
Ten Plagues of Egypt
Cloud Tabernacle
Imaculate Conception
Resurection of Jesus

8.

9. Chapters 2-7 because it is the Gentile History

10. Chapters 1-2, 8-12 because it pertains to the Israelites and end times

11. Troubled and disturbed

12.

13. That they tell him the dream and its interpretation

14. Prayed

15.

16. He told the King and praised and worshipped God

17. (Statue)
(Head) gold, King Neb., Babylonian Kingdom
(Chest) silver, Medo-Persian, Cyrus
(Belly & Thighs) bronze, Alexander the Great, Greece
(Legs) iron, Roman Empire, Julius Caesar
(Feet) iron and clay
(10 Toes) iron and clay, Revised Roman Empire-the EU, operating at the time of Christ's return

Chapter Three • Faith for Fiery Trials

1. Gold image - unity of Babylon and nation
Image of king - power and lust of the king

2.

3. Many differences, not prophetic, man's attempt at god status

4. 60 cubits high, 6 cubits wide - plain of Dura

5. When the music played they had to bow and worship the image of Nebuchadnezzar.

6. He is not on the Plain of Dura

7. Hananiah (Shadrach) Lord is gracious
Mishael   (Meshach) Wh is like God
Azariah   (Abednego) The Lord helps

8.

9. To keep their positions of influence
   Compromise as a victim of war

10. I formed you, created you, redeemed you, called you by name
When you pass through the waters –I am with you
When you pass through the rivers-they shall not overflow you
When you walk through the fire-you shall not be burned

11. YES

12. From the fire-miracle
Through the fire-going through
By fire –heaven

13. Example: From disease-miracle
Through sickness-remission
By fire-home to heaven

14. Our God can deliver us but if He doesn't, we won't bow!

15.Though tested by fire, we praise, honor and glorify Jesus.
Jesus endured the cross for the joy set before him.
Blessed is he who endures temptation to receive a crown of life.

In all things may God be glorified.
You will not be tempted above what you are able, but with
every temptation there is a way of escape.

16. Bound but loosed; 4th man walking, burned-no smell of
smoke on body, hair or clothing

17. Christophany-Pre-incarnate Christ

18. appeared
walked
instructed
feasted
wrestled
spoke
guided and provided for
shrouded
baby manger, crucified and resurrected
comforted
empowered
wept

Chapter Four • Finding God When You Have Lost Your Mind

1. He saw a tree full of lovely leaves and lush fruit and the beast
of the field were under it and birds nested in it. People were fed
by it. A watcher cried out, "Chop down the tree and strip it of it
branches, birds, leaves, fruit and animals." Bind with iron bands.
Let the tree be wet with dew and graze with beasts and have
the heart of a beast.

2. The tree is King Nebuchadnezzar who has grown great and
strong to heaven. They shall drive you from the palace and from
men. You will live like and eat the wet grass of the fields like an

animal for 7 years. Your kingdom will be restored to you when you honor God of Heaven.

3. In 12 months he said, "Is this not Babylon that I have built?" A voice from heaven said, "The Kingdom is departed from you."

4. Humble

5. God resists the proud but gives grace to the humble.

6. First dream-Chapter 2-He was head of gold on statue but would lose throne to Medes and Persians
Fiery furnace-Chapter 3 Hebrews delivered miraculously in the midst of fire.

7. The King's pride would cause his humiliation-lose his mind, throne, his reason, his sanity until he acknowledged the God of Heaven.

8. One full year

9. Angels watch and wait to administer commands of God

10. The iron band kept stump from splitting-restoration and growth still possible; not destroyed. Regrowth is now possible without parasite of pride.

11.

12.

13. In the Garden of Eden

14. Calvary, the cross

15. Righteous like a tree planted by the river of water
Fruit of righteousness is like a tree of life
Like days of a tree are days of my people
He is like a tree planted by water who sends out roots by the stream.

16.

17.

18. v. 2 - Signs and wonders has the Most High worked for me.
v.17 - Most High rules in the kingdom of men.
v.24 - This decree of the Most High which has come upon you
v.25 - 7 times pass over you till you know Most High rules in the kingdom of men
v.32 - 7 times pass over you till you know the Most High and give to whomever he chooses
v.34 - Neb. blessed the Most High and prayed, praised and honored him.

19.

20. Exactly as interpreted

21. 7 years

22. Praised God, Blessed God and Believed in God   Humiliation killed pride

Chapter 5 • Dead Man Walking

1. Daniel 1 - Daniel purposes not to defile himself or compromise his God.
Daniel 2 - Daniel with God's revelation interprets

Nebuchadnezzar's dream.
Daniel 3 - Three Hebrew men refuse to worship idol and God delivers them in the fire
Daniel 4 - Nebuchadnezzar, because of pride, is mentally ill 7 years and comes to know Jehovah

2. Belshazzar/Nabonicus

3. Belteshazzar

4. Nabonicus, Nebuchadnezzar, Daniel

5. Jonathan, Saul

6. Naomi, Ruth & Boaz

7. Fingers of a hand writing on the plaster wall of conquests

8. Face fell; countenance changed
Thoughts troubled him, joints of hips were loosened, knees knocked

9. In him dwelt the Spirit of the Holy God, he had understanding, wisdom, an excellent spirit, knowledge, and could interpret dreams and riddles

10. Drinking out of the holy anointed vessels of God

11. Medes and Persians diverted the Euphrates River and walked on dry river bed beneath walls unchallenged and killed King Belshazzar

12. Killed by soldiers

13.

14. God resists the proud but gives grace to the humble-brings down pride
Exalts the humble

15. Mene-God numbered the Kingdom and finished it
Mene
Tekel-you are weighed in the balances and found lacking
Uphrasin-kingdom divided and given to the Medes and Persians

16. Mene-your days are numbered and finished
Uphrasin-to divide and is dividing
Peres-divided and separated
Weighed, wanting, wicked

17. The walls were 60 miles in a perfect square (15 miles each side)
Walls 87 feet thick
Walls 350 feet high
Euphrates River flowed through the city

18. Moses took anointing oil and anointed tabernacle and everything in it
Consecrated all as holy; altar, utensils, laver, basin, and even Aaron and his sons

19. Defied what God had set aside as holy

20. Medes(Darius) and Persians (General Cyrus)

21.

22.

23. In an hour the uncontested army marched in and killed the king.

24. Medes and Persians

25. Darius-Mede and Cyrus-General

26. A decree was made to search the archives of the temple for the holy vessels

27. King Cyrus issued a decree to let the temple in Jerusalem be rebuilt and the gold and silver articles be restored to the temple and the people allowed to return.

28. 612 B.C. Nineveh, capital of Assyria, falls to General Nebuchadnezzar

605-Battle of Carchemish
Nebuchadnezzar defeats Egyptians
Nabopolassar - Neb. Father dies
Neb. captures Judah and becomes king

562 - Death of Nebachadnezzar

560-556 - Neriglassar - Merodach's Brother-in-law assassinated Merodach

555-539 - Nerigrassar's son ruled 2 months, assassinated by Nabonidus

539 - Nabonidus ruled 17 years and his son Belshazzar was co-regent (sometimes called Longimanus)

465-424 - Artaxexes King of Persia-son of Xerxes I – grandson of Darius-probably the same as Ahasuerus

Chapter 6 • Living With Lions

1. Fell in a single night without a battle on Oct. 12, 539 B.C.

2. Diverted Euphrates and entered under the walls on dry river bed; more importantly God ordained it

3. Verse 11 states 70 years

4.

5. Wonder of the world, impregnable, proud, arrogant, entitled, self absorbed

6. Daniel was a Hebrew slave who became boss over them. They thought it was unfair that he was promoted and not them. They felt they were more qualified, after all it was their land.

7. They were jealous of Daniel's relationship to King Darius and hated him because they could not find fault with him.

8. You would have no religious freedom for 30 days unless you worshipped him.

9. He prayed to the God of Israel 3 times a day, the same as always, in his home with the window open.

10. He was thrown in a den of lions.

11. It was a royal law and could not be changed. The king did not have absolute power.

12. He was safe, at peace and had a good night's rest.

13. No. He had no food, music, wine, women, rest and had a

guilty conscience

14. Yes. The Angel of the Lord closed the mouths of the lions

15.

16. Enoch-delivered from death

17. Noah-delivered from the flood

18. Moses-delivered from Pharaoh and Egypt

19. Joseph-delivered from slavery, prison and rejection

20. Same as always

21.

22.

23. Answered prayer, God's deliverance, justice of God on accusers, conversion of a king

24. The ones who intended for Daniel to be eaten by the lions were eaten themselves, their families also

25. Haman built huge gallows in order to hang Mordecai, but instead he and his family were hanged on that very gallows

Chapter 7 • The Coming World Leader

1.

2.

3. He is called little horn
King of a fierce countenance
Prince that will come
Rides on a white horse
Beast out of the sea
Man of sin, son of perdition
Wicked one
Antichrist

4.   1. Rapture of church
   2. Great tribulation
   3. Apocalypse of Antichrist
   4. Coming of Christ to earth
   5. All Israel saved
   6. Satan thrown in the bottomless pit
   7. Christ millennial reign

5. Is a leader who fulfills Biblical prophecies concerning an adversary of Christ, while resembling him in a deceptive manner.

6. Dragon - Satan mimics God
Beast - Satan's son mimics Jesus Christ
False Prophet - mimics the Holy Sprit

7. God visualized as human
Edict of judgment

8.

9.

10. Nations

11.

12. Satan

13. The Most High

14. Three and half years

15.

Chapter 8 • Power Shift Among Nations

1. Kingdom of Medes and Persians

2. Darius and Cyrus

3. Greece

4. Alexander the Great

5. Very young, malaria or alcoholism, 323 B.C.

6. Casander
Lysimachus
South and east Ptolemy
Antiochus Ephimanes, Seleucus

7. Glorious one, illustrious one, similar in type to Antichrist

8. Mad man

9. Israel

10. Run for your life

11. Sinister schemes (intrigue)

12. Many in their prosperity

13. He exalts himself and rides a pig in their temple

14. Destroys and deceives

Chapter 9 • The 70 Weeks Countdown

1. Jeremiah

2. Gabriel

3. To answer Daniel's prayer

4. Greatly beloved

5. John the Beloved-the disciple and Zechariah and Mary

6. Defending in writing or speech-defense of a belief.

7. Theology dealing with last things, death, resurrection, judgement, immortality.

8. Prediction of future under divine guidance.

9. Israel and Jerusalem

10. Finish

11. Rightousness

12. End

13. Seal up

14. Make reconciliation

15. Anoint

16. 49 years

17. 434 years

18. 7 years

19. Rebuild the city

20.

21. 173,880

22. Nehemiah asked King Artaxexes of Persia permission to go to rebuild Jerusalem and friends to pay for it. He said yes.

23. Cut off

24. The Jews rejected the 1st coming of Christ but to as many as believed on him, He gave right to be sons of God.

25. Israel

26. Puts his own image in the temple, declares himself to be God, stops everything regarding customs, sacrifices, kosher foods, circumcision

27.

28. Things horrible

29.

Chapter 10 • God's Glorious Touch

1. Preview of vision
Vision itself
Final instructions of vision

2. 3 years

3. Very distant

4. April 24

5. After Passover and end of Unleavened Bread

6. Affliction

7. Mourning for those who have gone back and for those who won't go back

8. Not many went, only 50,000

9.

10. Verses 13-15

11. Pre-incarnate Christ

12.

13.

14. He was at war with demonic Prince of Persia

15. He strengthened him and stood him up

16. Ruler of this world cast out
Ruler of this world is coming
Ruler of this world is judged

17. Archangel, protector of Israel

18. He gave him peace, strength, and no fear

19. Through the blood of the Lamb, the word of our testimony, not loving our lives more than our faith

20. Daniel was a man of prayer and could be trusted to keep the hidden mysteries and obey God.

Chapter 11 • Political Powers Unfolding

1. Angel

2. Did not

3. Our God is perfect and has a plan for everything He created. He is a just God, patient and long-suffering. He has made a way of escaping judgment

4. He was married to Queen Esther-an alien orphan Jewish girl in Persia. God used Esther to help spare the nation Israel from genocide at the hand of Hamon.

5. Alexander the Great

6. Macedonia West
   Thrace   North
   Egypt   South
   Syria   East

7. Syria
Antichrist
175 B.C.

8. He was a deceiver, liar, man full of blasphemies and hatred. He was full of vile actions.

9. "Against holy covenant" the people of God
"desecrated temple fortress" when treason and deceit fail.
Abolish daily sacrifice-worship torn down.
Abomination causes desolation-idol worship. He set up an altar to Zeus, He sacrificed a pig on the altar to make the temple unclean.

10. He was on the battlefield and was struck with a strange disease and suddenly died.

11. Antichrist
Antichrist
Tribulation

12.	Saves	Destroys
	Serves	Rules
	Leads in word & truth	Leads with spear and sword
	Is the son of God	Is the son of perdition (Satan)
	Brings love & peace	Brings hate & war
	Frees from sin	Enslaves to sin

13. Conquer the beautiful land Israel
Defeat God
Pretend to be God
Sit on God's throne
Abolish all worship to God
Set up his own throne on earth

14. Edom and Moab (Jordan)

15. Antichrist will set up headquarters between Mediterranean Sea and Jerusalem. He is destroyed by the personal return of Jesus Christ.

16. Abraham, Moses, David, Solomon, Daniel, Isaiah, Jonah, Jeremiah, Jacob, Melchizedek.

17. Antiochus Epiphanes

18.

19.

20.

21.

22. Resist

Chapter 12 • Our Prince Will Come

1.

2. Cast into the lake of fire.

3. They will be martyred and beheaded.

4. By the Tigris River.

5. Angels and the one in linen is the Lord Jesus Christ.

6. Jacob's trouble-the end of days, great and terrible day of the

Lord, time, times and a half time

7. They will be resurrected.

8.

9.

10.

11.

12. Raptured out

Everyone's Guide to
Demons & Spiritual Warfare

We are not powerless against evil. But to survive in our world today, we must know our real enemies and be fully aware of the resources and weapons we have to fight against them. This book is a basic training manual for understanding the war between good and evil and how to fight it.

Author: Ron M. Phillips

Publication Date: August 2010

Publishing House: Charisma House

ISBN: 9781616381271

To order go online,
www.ronphillips.org/store
Or call 1-800-877-6493

Our Invisible Allies

Beyond our normal range of understanding there lies another dimension more real and lasting than anything we can imagine. Angels are a key connection to that realm for us. Created by God, these timeless beings have a history and a story all their own.

In Our Invisible Allies, Ron Phillips brings you a definitive guide to angels, describing where they originated, how they operate, and how you can engage their help in your own life.

Author: Ron M. Phillips

Publication Date: October 2009

Publishing House: Charisma House

ISBN: 9781599795232

**To order go online,
www.ronphillips.org/store
Or call 1-800-877-6493**

Rooms of Her Heart:
Faith-Filled Living for Women

Within the pages of this practical book, Paulette Phillips creatively encourages women to allow God to inspect their inner lives room by room--the hallway of transition, the kitchen of hospitality, playroom of parenting, attic of hidden secrets, and more.

Author: Paulette Baker Phillips

Publication Date: 7/15/2004

Publishing House: Pathway Press

ISBN: 0871481359

**To order go online,
www.ronphillips.org/store
Or call 1-800-877-6493**

Esther:
Wrongs Made Right

Rebuilding Broken Families

If you are not suffering from some form of a broken or dysfunctional home, chances are that someone you love is. How can we diagnose the problems and rebuild our families? The only way is to return to God's guidelines for the family. In this compilation of material from Pastor Ron and Paulette Phillips, we'll examine the basis for the home life, marriage, and look at the foundations our homes and families should be built upon. You'll discover that intimacy with your spouse, coupled with intimacy with God, will shore up the shagging timbers of our home lives .

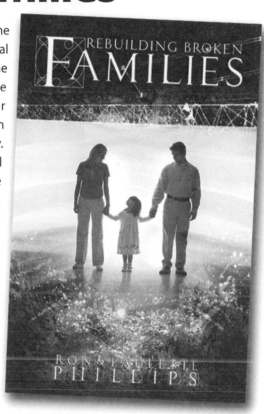

Author: Dr. Ron M. Phillips, Paulette Baker Phillips

Publication Date: 2009

Publishing House: Abba's House Publishing

ISBN: 9780979726828

**To order go online,
www.ronphillips.org/store
Or call 1-800-877-6493**

Secret of the Stairs:
Your Quest for Intimacy with Abba Father

Written almost entirely while away on a retreat of study and solitude, Ron Phillips draws you to discover hunger for something more in your walk with the Savior. God's Word is alive with men and women who came to an astounding realization of the Presence of the Most High, and Pastor Phillips examines their experiences, including David, Jacob, Isaiah, Elijah, Moses, Paul, and the beautiful picture of the lovers of Song of Solomon. Hardcover.

Author: Ron M. Phillips

Publication Date: 3/15/2006

Publishing House: World Publishing

ISBN: 0529122766

To order go online, www.ronphillips.org/store Or call 1-800-877-6493

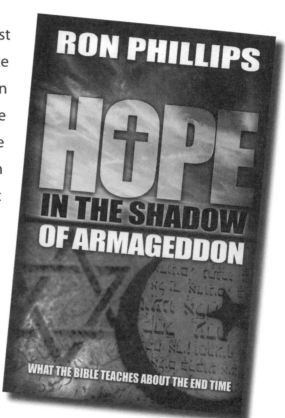

Vanquishing the Enemy:
Triumphant in the Battles of Life

Dr. Phillips' personal journey to spiritual freedom is found in the pages of this inspiring book. The balanced Biblical teaching is a powerful tool that can lead you on the path to spiritual victory.

Author: Dr. Ron M. Phillips

Publication Date: 4/27/1998

Publishing House: Pathway Press

ISBN: 0871488728

**To order go online,
www.ronphillips.org/store
Or call 1-800-877-6493**

Vanquishing the Enemy 2:
Moving to the Frontlines

This stirring release from Dr. Phillips calls the church to the next level of warfare against the forces of sin, providing valuable basic training to carry the Christian into spiritual battle with confidence.

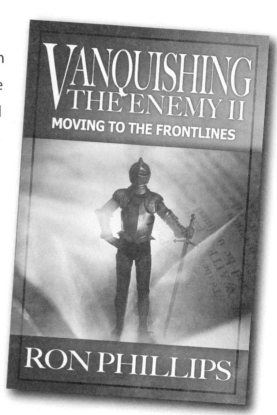

Author: Dr. Ron M. Phillips

Publication Date: 7/27/2004

Publishing House: Pathway Press

ISBN: 0-87148-146-4

To order go online, www.ronphillips.org/store Or call 1-800-877-6493

Awakened by the Spirit
Reclaiming the Forgotten Gift of God

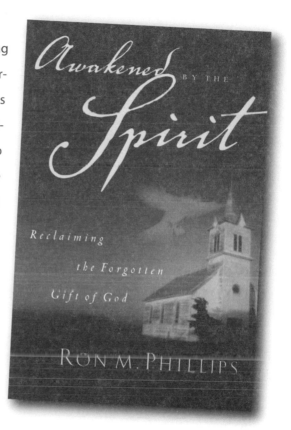

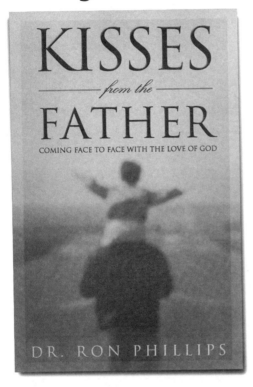